Current
CONTROVERSIES

D0796807

| LGBTQ Rights

Other Books in the Current Controversies Series

| LGBTQ Rights

Susan Henneberg, Book Editor

GREENHAVEN
PUBLISHING

Published in 2017 by Greenhaven Publishing, LLC
353 3rd Avenue, Suite 255, New York, NY 10010

Copyright © 2017 by Greenhaven Publishing, LLC

First Edition

Articles in Greenhaven Publishing anthologies are often edited for length to meet page
requirements. In addition, original titles of these works are changed to clearly present
the main thesis and to explicitly indicate the author's opinion. Every effort is made to
ensure that Greenhaven Publishing accurately reflects the original intent of the authors.
Every effort has been made to trace the owners of the copyrighted material.

Cover image: CHOKCHAI POOMICHAIYA/Shutterstock.com

Library of Congress Cataloging-in-Publication Data

Names: Henneberg, Susan, editor.
Title: LGBTQ rights / edited by Susan Henneberg.
Description: New York : Greenhaven Publishing, 2017. |
Series: Current controversies | Includes index.
Identifiers: LCCN ISBN 9781534500358 (pbk.) | ISBN 9781534500198 (library bound)
Subjects: LCSH: Gay rights--Juvenile literature. | Sexual minorities--Political
activity--Juvenile literature. | Identity politics--Juvenile literature.
Classification: LCC HQ76.5 H46 2017 | DDC 323.3'264--dc23

Manufactured in the United States of America

Website: http://greenhavenpublishing.com

Contents

Chapter 1: Does the LGBTQ Community Enjoy Equal Rights?

Arwen Armbrecht

LGBTQ rights, such as same-sex marriage, are improving in North America and Europe. However, LGBTQ people still suffer from discrimination and marginalization. Many nations in the world still criminalize homosexual behavior. Legislation and education are important tools for achieving equal rights for LGBTQ people.

Yes: The LGBTQ Community Enjoys Equal Rights

Ian Millhiser

The State of Ohio is petitioning the Supreme Court to allow it to practice marriage discrimination. State attorneys claim that LGBTQ people have too much political power to need the "heightened scrutiny" awarded to populations who have historically been subject to irrational discrimination and are politically powerless. Rather, LGBTQ communities have won significant rights over the last few years.

Genny Beemyn

There is a lot of work yet to be done, but LGBTQ rights have come a long way. Given the remarkably rapid recent developments in recognition of the trans community in particular, there is every reason to be hopeful about improvements to the rights of transgender individuals around the world.

Chapter 3: Is Same-Sex Marriage a Human Right?

Chapter 4: Do Transgender Individuals Deserve Special Protection?

Foreword

C ontroversy" is a word that has an undeniably unpleasant connotation. It carries a definite negative charge. Controversy can spoil family gatherings, spread a chill around classroom and campus discussion, inflame public discourse, open raw civic wounds, and lead to the ouster of public officials. We often feel that controversy is almost akin to bad manners, a rude and shocking eruption of that which must not be spoken or thought of in polite, tightly guarded society. To avoid controversy, to quell controversy, is often seen as a public good, a victory for etiquette, perhaps even a moral or ethical imperative.

Yet the studious, deliberate avoidance of controversy is also a whitewashing, a denial, a death threat to democracy. It is a false sterilizing and sanitizing and superficial ordering of the messy, ragged, chaotic, at times ugly processes by which a healthy democracy identifies and confronts challenges, engages in passionate debate about appropriate approaches and solutions, and arrives at something like a consensus and a broadly accepted and supported way forward. Controversy is the megaphone, the speaker's corner, the public square through which the citizenry finds and uses its voice. Controversy is the life's blood of our democracy and absolutely essential to the vibrant health of our society.

Our present age is certainly no stranger to controversy. We are consumed by fierce debates about technology, privacy, political correctness, poverty, violence, crime and policing, guns, immigration, civil and human rights, terrorism, militarism, environmental protection, and gender and racial equality. Loudly competing voices are raised every day, shouting opposing opinions, putting forth competing agendas, and summoning starkly different visions of a utopian or dystopian future. Often these voices attempt to shout the others down; there is precious little listening and considering among the cacophonous din. Yet listening and considering, too, are essential to the health of a democracy. If controversy is democracy's lusty lifeblood, respectful listening and careful thought are its higher faculties, its brain, its conscience.

Current Controversies does not shy away from or attempt to hush the loudly competing voices. It seeks to provide readers with as wide and representative as possible a range of articulate voices on any given controversy of the day, separates each one out to allow it to be heard clearly and fairly, and encourages careful listening to each of these well-crafted, thoughtfully expressed opinions, supplied by some of today's leading academics, thinkers, analysts, politicians, policy makers, economists, activists, change agents, and advocates. Only after listening to a wide range of opinions on an issue, evaluating the strengths and weaknesses of each argument, assessing how well the facts and available evidence mesh with the stated opinions and conclusions, and thoughtfully and critically examining one's own beliefs and conscience can the reader begin to arrive at his or her own conclusions and articulate his or her own stance on the spotlighted controversy.

This process is facilitated and supported in each Current Controversies volume by an introduction and chapter overviews that provide readers with the essential context they need to begin engaging with the spotlighted controversies, with the debates surrounding them, and with their own perhaps shifting or nascent opinions on them. Chapters are organized around several key questions that are answered with diverse opinions representing all points on the political spectrum. In its content, organization, and methodology, readers are encouraged to determine the authors' point of view and purpose, interrogate and analyze the various arguments and their rhetoric and structure, evaluate the arguments' strengths and weaknesses, test their claims against available facts and evidence, judge the validity of the reasoning, and bring into clearer, sharper focus the reader's own beliefs and conclusions and how they may differ from or align with those in the collection or those of classmates.

Research has shown that reading comprehension skills improve dramatically when students are provided with compelling, intriguing, and relevant "discussable" texts. The subject matter of these collections could not be more compelling, intriguing, or urgently relevant to today's students and the world they are poised to inherit. The anthologized articles also provide the basis for stimulating, lively, and passionate classroom debates. Students who are compelled to anticipate objections to their own argument and identify the flaws in those of an opponent read more carefully, think more critically, and steep themselves in relevant context, facts, and information more thoroughly. In short, using discussable text of the kind provided by every single volume in the Current Controversies series encourages close reading, facilitates reading comprehension, fosters research, strengthens critical thinking, and greatly enlivens and energizes classroom discussion and participation. The entire learning process is deepened, extended, and strengthened.

If we are to foster a knowledgeable, responsible, active, and engaged citizenry, we must provide readers with the intellectual, interpretive, and critical-thinking tools and experience necessary to make sense of the world around them and of the all-important debates and arguments that inform it. We must encourage them not to run away from or attempt to quell controversy but to embrace it in a responsible, conscientious, and thoughtful way, to sharpen and strengthen their own informed opinions by listening to and critically analyzing those of others. This series encourages respectful engagement with and analysis of current controversies and competing opinions and fosters a resulting increase in the strength and rigor of one's own opinions and stances. As such, it helps readers assume their rightful place in the public square and provides them with the skills necessary to uphold their awesome responsibility—guaranteeing the continued and future health of a vital, vibrant, and free democracy.

Introduction

> *"The Constitution promises liberty*
> *to all within its reach, a liberty that*
> *includes certain specific rights that*
> *allow persons, within a lawful realm,*
> *to define and express their identity."*
>
> Justice Anthony Kennedy

Nebraska resident Luke Peterson loved and was well-qualified for his job at a Lincoln wine shop. The day after his boyfriend stopped by to see the shop, Peterson was told he wasn't needed at work anymore, Peterson told the Human Rights Campaign (HRC), a national nonprofit organization working for LGBTQ civil rights. In a similar situation, successful Texas real estate agent Carter Brown was fired from his job soon after a colleague outed him as transgender to his employer. These are not isolated cases. Nearly two-thirds of LGBTQ Americans have experienced discrimination in employment, housing, access to public places, adoption, and other areas, according to a 2015 HRC poll.

Many people thought that because of the historic Supreme Court ruling in *Obergefell v. Hodges* in 2015, full LGBTQ rights had been achieved. However, *Obergefell* concerned only the right to marry. The named plaintiff was Ohio resident James Obergefell, who married his partner in Maryland where same-sex marriage was legal. When his spouse died, officials in Ohio refused to recognize the marriage on the death certificate. Obergefell sued to get his marriage recognized by the state of Ohio. The defendant was Richard Hodges, Ohio's health director. Eventually, sixteen same-sex couples combined their cases as they worked their way through federal circuit and appeals courts. On June 26, 2015, the US Supreme Court decided in a 5–4 split that the Fourteenth Amendment requires all states to grant same-sex marriages. "The Constitution promises liberty to all within its reach," Justice Anthony Kennedy wrote in the majority opinion, "a liberty that includes certain specific rights that allow persons, within a lawful realm, to define and express their identity."

The specific rights referred to by Justice Kennedy were confined to marriage. The historic decision does not guarantee the civil rights enjoyed by most Americans, many LGBTQ people and their supporters claim. Gay, lesbian, bisexual, and transsexual citizens continue to face discrimination on many fronts. For instance, it is still legal in many places for employers to fire workers based on sexual orientation or gender identity. In many states, transgender citizens are prevented from using the restrooms that correspond to their gender identity. LGBTQ people face discrimination from housing providers. When 49 people were killed and 53 others were wounded in a massacre at a gay nightclub in Orlando, Florida, gay and bisexual men were prevented from donating blood for victims.

To address issues of discrimination against LGBTQ citizens, various states and some municipalities have passed a patchwork of laws banning discrimination based on sexual orientation and gender identity. In 2015, a group of US House of Representatives and Senate Democrats introduced a bill called the Equality Act, which would expand the 1964 Civil Rights Act to explicitly protect people from discrimination because of sexual orientation or gender identity. Many LGBTQ people feared that the bill would not pass without the support of social conservatives in Congress. LGBTQ leaders such as National Center for Lesbian Rights executive director Kate Kendell warned after the Supreme Court same-sex marriage decision that a backlash against LGBTQ equality laws might follow.

What many LGBTQ people called a backlash against same-sex marriage equality appeared to sweep through the nation in 2015 and 2016. HRC reported that 200 anti-LGBTQ bills were introduced in thirty-four states. The proposed bills, some of which were passed, allowed businesses to cite religion as a legal reason to refuse goods or services to LGBTQ people. The state bills blocked the ability of local government to pass anti-discrimination ordinances. The rights of transgender people received particular attention. Some states passed what became known as "bathroom bills." These laws required transgender people to use public bathrooms that corresponded to the gender on their birth certificate. The status of transgender Americans received new media attention. According to the National Center for Transgender Equality, transgender people suffer from high suicide rates, high rates of homelessness and unemployment, and an "epidemic of anti-trans violence."

Full equality for LGBTQ people has become a subject of controversy not only in the US but worldwide. Many people in the international LGBTQ community argue that the right for same-sex couples to marry is a human right, as established by the Universal Declaration of Human Rights (UDHR) in 1947. As of 2015, almost two dozen nations allowed same-sex marriage. In much of the world, however LGBTQ citizens are victims of discrimination, inequality, violence, and abuse. The United Nations Human Rights Council adopted a resolution on June 30, 2016, which conferred "protection against violence and discrimination based on sexual orientation and gender identity." The council mandated the appointment of an independent expert to assist nations in implementing human rights laws toward LGBTQ citizens. The vote of the council was not unanimous, and many countries resist changing discriminatory laws and violent attitudes.

The articles in this book focus on the status of equal rights for LGBTQ people in the US and worldwide. Readers will learn about gains and losses in chapters titled "Does the LGBTQ Community Enjoy Equal Rights?" "Does the Promotion of LGBTQ Rights Threaten the Freedom of Others?" "Is Same-Sex Marriage a Human Right?" and "Do Transgender Individuals Deserve Special Protection?" These chapters provide a variety of issues and viewpoints from which readers can make up their own minds about the answers to these important questions.

Does the LGBTQ Community Enjoy Equal Rights?

Overview: LGBTQ Rights Are Improving Around the World

Arwen Armbrecht

Arwen Armbrecht is a freelance writer and social media producer.

L ast year saw a set of victories for the LGBT community, both in the United States and Europe. The call for a more diverse and inclusive world is gaining momentum, but it is important to remember that while diversity is becoming more widespread, there is a great deal of work still to be done for LGBT rights around the world.

What does LGBT mean?

LGBT is the most commonly used acronym for the lesbian, gay, bisexual and transgender community. This umbrella term is in fact the shorter version of a wide variety of other acronyms which are used to be more inclusive of other individuals. The list of possibilities subject to some debate. Sometimes an "I" is added to include intersex (people with the physical characteristics of both genders), and sometimes a "Q" for people who identify simply as queer. There are many other communities within LGBT such as (but not exclusively confined to) asexuals (people who are not attracted to anyone in a sexual manner or do not have a sexual orientation), pansexuals (people who are sexually attracted to all or a wide variety of gender identifications) and non-binary (people whose gender identities are not exclusively masculine or feminine) people.

"Explainer: The State of LGBT Rights Today," Arwen Armbrecht, January 4, 2016. Reprinted by permission.

What kind of problems do LGBT people face around the world?

The struggles of LGBT people vary dramatically around the world. While people living in the west have made massive strides in achieving equal rights, there are still many countries where gay marriage is still not recognised, and in some countries homosexual relationships are still punishable by death.

The right to marry

Around the world, there are 23 countries where same-sex marriage is legal. The majority of nations are in the Americas and Europe, with South Africa and New Zealand also on the list. In the UK, gay marriage is devolved to national parliaments, so is only legal in England, Wales and Scotland. In Mexico only certain jurisdictions have legalised same-sex marriage.

"Gay-friendly" nations and LGBT rights

While same-sex marriage is a strong indicator of nations opening up to the LGBT community, it does not guarantee that those nations are "gay-friendly" in a broader sense. In the United States, for example, numerous political candidates for the 2016 presidential elections are running on a platform of removing same-sex marriage and other LGBT protections.

Europe is arguably the most "gay-friendly" continent. When asked which countries were most gay-friendly, a recent survey showed that 8 out of the top ten were in Europe.

Nevertheless, Europe as a whole still has much work to do. In May 2015, ILGA released its LGBT equality ratings. The UK and Belgium lead the continent with over 80% of full equality achieved in both countries. Much of western Europe also achieves high levels of equality, but as the map moves further east, those numbers begin to plummet.

Same-sex relationships are still criminalised—or even punishable by death

There are many places in the world where being LGBT is not only illegal but punishable by death. The data on what is specifically happening to LGBT individuals in a given country of persecution is sometimes difficult to verify. In countries such as as Nigeria and Somalia, for example, there is evidence of the execution of LGBT people, even though homosexuality is not officially punishable by death. Regions controlled by ISIS are particularly brutal in their methods of execution towards LGBT people.

Mauritania, Sudan, Iran, Saudi Arabia and Yemen all have active legislation leading to the death penalty for LGBT people.

Is the situation improving?

In the west, LGBT rights continue to improve. Better education, changing cultural norms and the growing evidence of the economic benefits of diversity have all contributed to a more inclusive environment for LGBT people.

Changes in legislation and LGBT portrayal in the media are important, but a change in cultural attitudes must also follow. Despite Europe's progress, a 2012 report from the European Union Agency for Fundamental Rights showed that 47% of LGBT people had reported being the victims of harassment. Lesbian women in particular were targets (55%) as were people in lower income (52%) brackets.

This kind of cultural discrimination has an economic impact. One in five people reported being discriminated against in the workplace in 2012, while one in eight said that it had an impact on their seeking employment. That number soars to one in three for transgender people.

The most important lesson for progress in the west will be to remember that we are not yet finished.

In other parts of the world, however, the outlook is substantially less encouraging. In numerous countries, LGBT people have been discriminated against for political gain.

What is the cost of discrimination?

Discrimination against LGBT people is not a community issue, it is both a national and human issue. Mental health issues and suicide rates continue to be higher among LGBT persons than in other communities. In addition to the toll discrimination can take on a community, non-inclusive work environments have been shown to have a strong impact on productivity in the workplace.

In their 2014 report, The Economic Cost of Homophobia: A Case Study of India, the World Bank found that the Indian economy was losing as much as 1.7% of its GDP due to homophobia. The loss of labor force and shrunken productivity has been shown to cause a ripple effect.

Free and Equal, an initiative of the United Nations, explains that in a study of 39 countries, the marginalisation of the LGBT community was causing a substantial loss of potential economic output. In an economy the size of India's, as much as 32 billion dollars a year are lost, resulting in a drag on growth and lower tax revenues, which in turn damages education and health funding.

What can be done to push forwards on LGBT rights?

Discrimination can be stopped, both through legislation and education. The European Union, for example, has set out a ten point plan for improving the understanding of LGBT issues, particularly among youth, as well as passing stronger universal diversity laws. Creating a safe and welcoming workspace is also a key factor in ensuring LGBT inclusiveness. Every year, the campaigning organisation OUTstanding presents a list of executives who are working to that end.

The state of LGBT rights, and what can be done by both the business community and governments, will be discussed at the World Economic Forum's Annual Meeting in Davos later his month.

The LGBTQ Community Has Political Power

Ian Millhiser

Ian Millhiser is justice editor of ThinkProgress, a political news blog affiliated with the Center for American Progress, a progressive public policy research and advocacy organization.

G ay Americans simply have too much political power to be afforded equal rights under the Constitution, according to a brief filed by the state of Ohio asking the Supreme Court to permit that state to continue to practice marriage discrimination. Ohio's claim comes as part of a greater effort to convince the justices that laws which discriminate again gay men, lesbians and bisexuals should not be treated with skepticism by courts applying the Constitution's guarantee that everyone shall be afforded "the equal protection of the laws."

Under this provision of the Constitution, most forms of discrimination are entirely permissible. It is acceptable, for example, for the government to discriminate against unqualified job applicants when making hiring decisions, or to discriminate against people who commit serious crimes in deciding who to incarcerate.

When the government discriminates against groups that have historically been subject to unequal treatment that has little basis in their ability to "perform or contribute to society," however, the Court applies what is known as "heightened scrutiny" to such discrimination. This is why discrimination on the basis of race or gender is typically not allowed, because racial minorities and women have historically been subject to the kind of irrational discrimination that triggers heightened scrutiny. A major question in the marriage equality litigation now pending before the

"State Attorneys Tell Supreme Court that Gay People Are Too Powerful to Have Equal Rights," Ian Millhiser, March 30, 2015. Reprinted by permission.

Supreme Court is whether the nation's long history of irrational discrimination against gay people also justifies applying such scrutiny to laws that discriminate on the basis of sexual orientation.

Though the answer to this question is not dispositive of whether a group should be afforded heightened protection under the Constitution, the Supreme Court has, at times, asked whether that group has been "relegated to such a position of political powerlessness as to command extraordinary protection from the majoritarian political process" when determining which groups should receive this protection. Ohio argues that such protection is unwarranted because, in recent years, gay people have started to win battles in the political arena:

At the federal level, the executive branch filed an amicus brief, as did some 167 Representatives and 44 Senators. Not only that, with respect to DOMA, the executive branch's strong support led it to the "unusual position" of failing "to defend the constitutionality of an Act of Congress based on a constitutional theory not yet established in judicial decisions" and that was rejected by four Justices. At the state level, 19 States filed four amicus briefs in these cases challenging the laws of their sister sovereigns. Further, several state officers have, like the federal government, "refused to defend" their own laws. At the local level, some 226 Mayors and many of the largest cities expressed support.

It is true that a minority of states and a minority of both houses of Congress filed briefs supporting marriage equality, as did an executive branch led by the only president in American history to openly support marriage equality while in office. But if that were sufficient reason to prevent same-sex couples from seeking relief in court, then the Constitution would also cease affording heightened protection to racial minorities and to women.

As I explain in my new book, *Injustices: The Supreme Court's History of Comforting the Comfortable and Afflicting the Afflicted*, the Supreme Court barely enforced the Constitution's protections against race discrimination for decades after the Fourteenth Amendment was ratified. The Court mostly stood silent as Southern states embraced apartheid through Jim Crow laws, eventually upholding segregation itself in *Plessy v. Ferguson.* Chinese residents faced similar discrimination in California. Japanese Americans were rounded up and placed in internment camps during World War II—with the blessing of the Supreme Court.

The justices did not really begin to enforce the Constitution's bar on racial apartheid until *Brown v. Board of Education.* And, as I lay out in *Injustices*, the Court did not enforce *Brown* itself with any real vigor until 1964—the same year that civil rights leaders exerted enough political clout to pass a major anti-discrimination bill through Congress.

The implication of Ohio's argument is that groups seeking to invoke the Constitution's guarantee of equality must bring a lawsuit during a kind of Goldilocks period—when the group simultaneously has amassed enough clout to earn the justices' sympathies, but without amassing so much clout that they are only permitted to appeal to the political branches. But the Court's civil rights cases have never insisted on this kind of Goldilocks rule.

Indeed, Ohio's suggestion that courts should not extend marriage equality to groups that have achieved a degree of political power is repudiated by the Supreme Court's first marriage equality decision, *Loving v. Virginia. Loving*, which barred racial marriage discrimination, was decided in 1967—three years after the Civil Rights Act of 1964 barred race discrimination in employment and in public accommodations such as restaurants. As recent events in Indiana remind us, gay Americans do not yet enjoy these same rights to work and to patronize businesses free from discrimination. But the fact that racial minorities had already achieved significant legislative victories by 1967 did not strip them of the protections they also enjoy under the Constitution.

The same can be said about women. The Civil Rights Act of 1964 also prohibits many forms of gender discrimination, but the Supreme Court did not hand down its first decision recognizing that the Constitution also protects against gender discrimination until its 1971 decision in *Reed v. Reed.* Again, the Civil Rights

Act grants women and racial minorities legal protections that gay people still do not enjoy to this very day, at least at the federal level. So if gay Americans have somehow acquired so much power that they should no longer be able to seek refuge in the Constitution, *Loving* and *Reed* were both wrongly decided.

Two years ago, House Republicans made a similar gay-people-are-too-powerful argument in their brief supporting the anti-gay Defense of Marriage Act (DOMA). That brief claimed that "gays and lesbians are one of the most influential, best-connected, best-funded, and best organized interest groups in modern politics, and have attained more legislative victories, political power, and popular favor in less time than virtually any other group in American history." This argument did not carry the day in *United States v. Windsor*, the decision striking down DOMA (though it is worth noting that *Windsor* also did not establish that anti-gay discrimination is subject to heightened scrutiny). If the Court follows its own decisions, the argument that gay people have amassed too much political clout to have equal rights will not carry the day in Ohio's case either.

LGBTQ Individuals Have Reasons to Cheer

Genny Beemyn

Genny Beemyn is the director of the UMass Amherst Stonewall Center and the coordinator of the Trans Policy Clearinghouse for Campus Pride, a national LGBTQ youth advocacy organization.

Editor's note: This article is part of our collaboration with Point Taken, a new program from WGBH that next airs on Tuesday, May 24 on PBS and online at pbs.org. The show features fact-based debate on major issues of the day, without the shouting.

There is a long way to go before transgender people throughout the United States are treated with respect and dignity, as shown by the opposition in some places to trans people using restrooms that match their gender identity. A number of states and school districts have taken a stand against the Obama administration's reading of Title VII and Title IX—amendments that prohibit discrimination on the basis of gender identity and sexual orientation—as applying to transgender people too.

But as a scholar on the experiences of young trans people, I believe my research suggests that it is only a matter of time before trans people achieve equal rights and wider social acceptance. While gender is different from sexuality, the history of the struggle for same-sex marriage in this country shows why this will be the case.

From social outlaws to family in-laws

Prior to the year 2000, no state recognized same-sex marriages or even civil unions. At the time, the federal government also defined marriage as a union between one man and one woman. Public opinion polls indicated that a clear majority of heterosexual people in the U.S. opposed the recognition of same-sex relationships.

By 2011, six states had legalized same-sex marriages, and national opinion polls showed an equal split between those in favor and those opposed on the issue. And by the time of the Supreme Court's ruling in 2015 that legalized same-sex marriage throughout the country, proponents led opponents, according to the Pew Research Center, by 16 percentage points. The ruling was heralded by President Obama, who had "evolved" to become supportive. The White House, where Democratic President Bill Clinton had signed a law banning federal recognition of same-sex marriages, was lit up in the colors of the rainbow flag.

How did such a dramatic change occur in a little more than 15 years?

Foremost, it was the demographic power of millennials that led to changes in opinion polls—a trend that policymakers could not ignore. Millennials generally see same-sex marriage as a basic civil rights issue and back it by a wide margin. Older generations have also become more supportive during the last decade, but by a much lesser degree. This means, demographically, the number of individuals who are supportive will grow over time, while members of older generations, who are generally less supportive, will pass away.

Support for the issue among heterosexual millennials was largely based on their knowing individuals who self-disclosed to them as lesbian, gay or bisexual—friends, coworkers and sometimes partners. The issue became personal.

Research has consistently found that heterosexual, cisgender (non-transgender) people in the U.S. who know a lesbian, gay, bisexual or transgender individual are generally more supportive of that particular group and their rights.

It is difficult to deny the humanity of a group of people if someone close to you belongs to that group. And according to a 2015 Pew Research Center poll, 90 percent of heterosexual millennials report personally knowing someone who identifies as lesbian or gay. That includes 58 percent who have a close friend or family member who is out to them as lesbian or gay.

To know us is to at least like us

Trans people are just beginning to benefit from this support-by-personal-contact effect because there are seemingly fewer of us than cisgender lesbian, gay and bisexual people—and fewer of us are out.

A 2011 Williams Institute study placed the number of LGBT people in the United States at approximately nine million, of which about 700,000 are transgender. In terms of U.S. adolescents, estimates suggest between one-half percent and 1.5 percent are transgender, whereas estimates of cisgender LGBQ youth range from 4 percent to 9 percent.

As reflected in schools and colleges throughout the country, a growing number of young people are coming out as trans. But many others are not out, or out to only a few cisgender family members, friends and colleagues, because the climate has often been hostile for trans people. A national study I conducted for a book I am writing on LGBTQ+ college students found that only about half of the students who identify outside of a gender binary were out to a parent.

According to a 2015 Harris poll, just 16 percent of non-LGBT people say that they personally know someone who identifies as transgender. While this figure is double the percent found in a 2008 study, it pales in comparison to that 90 percent figure for knowing someone lesbian or gay. For many cisgender individuals, trans people will remain a scary, amorphous danger until they knowingly have direct experiences with trans people.

There is a catch-22 here.

If more trans people were out, it would help improve the political and social climate for us. However, many trans people understandably do not want to self-disclose, if they can avoid it, because the current climate is often hostile. Trans individuals who are out now, many of whom are young people, regularly encounter harassment and microaggressions, such as being misgendered and verbally and physically attacked in bathrooms.

But, at the same time, young, out trans people are bringing about changes in cisgender people's attitudes that will help ensure trans individuals in the future will have equal rights and not experience this level of discrimination.

According to a 2015 Human Rights Campaign survey, for example, 66 percent of cisgender individuals who said they know a transgender person expressed supportive feelings toward them, as compared to 37 percent support among cisgender individuals who indicated that they do not know a transgender person.

Trans college students

My own research on transgender college students who have come out describes the struggles they must overcome to be treated with dignity on their campus. While some trans students find their college has policies in place to support them, most discover that their institution denies them the ability to feel safe and fully be themselves.

Few colleges formally acknowledge and respect transgender students by, for example, recognizing the first name that trans individuals use for themselves, providing a nonmedical means to switch the M/F gender marker on campus records, or enabling them to be recognized as neither M/F. Only about 150 colleges enable trans students to change their name on campus records without having to make changes to legal documents, and only about 50 will change the gender marker without students having to making legal changes.

Similarly, colleges that do not provide gender-inclusive bathrooms, housing or locker rooms signal to trans students, whether intentionally or unintentionally, that they should not be out and are not welcomed at the institution. The lack of administrative support for trans students creates a negative campus climate. This is exacerbated by the failure of colleges to require students, staff and faculty to attend an educational session to address discrimination against trans people, as is commonly done to counter sexual harassment.

The inclusion of gender identity and expression under Title IX's prohibition against sex discrimination will make campuses more trans-inclusive over time. The law requires colleges to treat trans students in accordance with their identity and gives them recourse if they experience harassment or discrimination because of their gender identity or expression.

But laws and policies can only do so much. Transgender people and cisgender supporters will still need to push institutions and society at large to change and understand that gender is not a binary. This is gradually happening.

While open opposition to trans people being treated in keeping with their gender identity is increasing, so too is support. For example, the passage of North Carolina's anti-transgender bathroom law has led to a boycott of the state by a growing list of businesses, other state and city governments, national organizations and musicians.

A recent national opinion poll finds that almost 60 percent of people in the U.S. oppose laws like the one in North Carolina. That same poll indicates that three-quarters of cisgender people support laws guaranteeing equal protection for transgender individuals.

It took 15 years to bring about a sea change on same-sex marriage. Transgender equality nationwide is not only a matter of time, but it is likely to happen faster.

The LGBTQ Community Still Suffers from Injustices

David Miller

David Miller is a doctoral student in psychology at Northwestern University.

When I came out as gay in my sophomore year of college, I absolutely loved going to Tigerheat—a kitschy 18-and-over gay club in Los Angeles. I mostly remember my nights there as frivolous fun, but they also had deeper meaning. That's where I first learned how to openly and unabashedly celebrate being gay.

I danced wildly to Britney Spears in the fog and strobe lights, made out with beautiful men and bonded with college friends who came along. After hiding my sexual orientation for nearly a decade, those moments liberated me. After isolating myself from other gay people for years, I was suddenly surrounded by them. Those nights had special meaning to me as someone exploring my newfound identity as an openly gay man.

Such memories make me especially disgusted that a gay club has become the site of the U.S.'s deadliest mass shooting ever. An assailant who apparently hated gay people shot over 100 people at the Orlando gay club Pulse. A space created as a respite from discrimination had turned into the setting for a horrific nightmare.

As this massacre reminds us, violent hatred toward lesbian, gay, bisexual and transgender (LGBT) people still remains in the United States. LGBT people also still do not have full equal legal rights under U.S. law, despite winning marriage rights, and face daily stressors and fears that others do not. Fortunately, however,

"LGBT Equality Doesn't Exist—But Here's How to Fight for It," David Miller, The Conversation, June 15, 2016. http://theconversation.com/LGBT-equality-doesnt-exist-but -heres-how-to-fight-for-it-60977. Licensed under CC BY ND International 4.0.

social science research has begun to identify concrete actions to durably erode such hatred and create environments inclusive to LGBT people.

Injustices against LGBT people

LGBT people are more likely than any other minority group, including black people and Muslims, to be targeted in a violent hate crime, according to a 2011 Southern Poverty Law Center analysis of FBI statistics. LGBT people of color face particularly high rates of violence. For instance, at least 21 transgender women were murdered in the U.S. in 2015, and 19 of those 21 were women of color.

The injustices against the LGBT community extend well beyond unconscionable, violent hate crimes. For instance, in a large 2013 national survey of middle school and high school students, 65 percent of LGBT students reported hearing homophobic remarks like "fag" or "dyke" frequently or often, and 30 percent missed at least one day of school in the previous month because they felt unsafe or uncomfortable.

Compared to the general population, LGBT people also face higher rates of homelessness, depression and suicide, especially among transgender people. For instance, national surveys estimate that between 25 and 43 percent of transgender adults have attempted suicide at some point in their life, compared to 10 to 20 percent of LGB adults and 5 percent of the general U.S. population.

Though declining over time, homophobic attitudes are still with us in the U.S. For instance, according to Gallup poll data, 37 percent of Americans still view "gay or lesbian relations" as morally wrong, compared to 53 percent of Americans in 2001. And despite this modest decline in explicitly stated homophobia, seeing two men or two women kiss still disgusts many people—even well-intentioned people—at an implicit, automatic level.

Anti-LGBT bias intersects with others

These harsh realities remind me how much of a protected bubble I live in as a young white cisgender male graduate student living in Chicago's largest gay neighborhood. Being physically attacked for my gender presentation or even my sexual orientation is not a daily fear for me, but it can be for transgender people simply trying to use the bathroom.

Multiple factors such as gender, race and geographic location intersect to shape prejudice in complex ways. For instance, as photographer and writer Samra Habib described, many queer Muslims not only fear homophobic attacks but also "have to take extra care walking down the street at night and entering [their] mosques for fear of Islamophobic attacks."

The racial targeting of the Orlando victims also can't be overlooked. The assailant who reportedly hated races and religions other than his own attacked the gay club on its "Latin Night." The victims, including Edward Sotomayor, Amanda Alvear, Eddie Jamoldroy Justice, Deonka Deidra Drayton and too many others, were primarily Latino, Hispanic or black.

Using policy to fight for LGBT equality

One positive outcome of this tragedy is a sharp, rude awakening that the fight for full LGBT equality is far from over. Even members of the LGBT community such as myself can at times forget and become complacent about this reality.

Part of the fight can be won through policy change. Despite the Supreme Court's historic gay marriage ruling in June 2015, LGBT people still do not have equal legal rights in the U.S. For instance, in 28 states, private employers can still legally fire employees based on sexual orientation or gender identity. Those same 28 states also provide no explicit protections against LGBT discrimination in housing; that's especially dismaying because large field experiments have found bias against gay couples inquiring about apartment rentals and senior housing.

A proposed bill in Congress called the Equality Act would amend the 1964 Civil Rights Act and ban LGBT discrimination in employment, housing, public education, access to credit, jury service and public accommodations such as restrooms and stores in all 50 states and Washington, D.C. Over 85 percent of Democratic members of Congress have formally endorsed the bill, but Republicans have actively blocked it.

If enacted, such policy changes could have cascading effects on attitudes and behaviors. For instance, a 2013 study in Texas found that city-level bans on employment discrimination based on sexual orientation made employers treat presumed gay applicants more favorably in a real or mock interview hiring context.

Those laws influenced behavior not because employers feared punishment, the study's researchers argued, but instead because the laws set the morals of the community. "Even absent any possibility of tangible punishment, legislation may reduce a given act (discrimination) simply by designating it as illegal, criminal, or deviant," the researchers suggested. However, researchers haven't yet empirically verified this psychological mechanism in this context.

Using conversations to fight for LGBT equality

Everyday citizens can fight for LGBT equality by voting for politicians who will push for pro-LGBT policies. However, short face-to-face conversations can also help durably change LGBT attitudes. Although scientists have been suspicious about such claims because of an earlier scandal involving faked data, other independent researchers with new data are finding real results.

In a recently published study in Science, 10 minutes of conversation about transgender rights reduced transphobic attitudes for at least three months. In the study, 56 canvassers knocked on the doors of 501 voters in Miami.

To avoid effects that are only short-lived, as found in some prior studies, canvassers actively engaged voters in conversation about voters' personal views and experiences. For instance, voters were asked to consider a time in which they were judged for being different and then consider how transgender people might encounter similar experiences. Compared to passively listening to well-rehearsed arguments, such active learning approaches have often been far more effective at durably reducing prejudice.

This study's results should be reproduced before they are considered robust. However, if they do replicate and transfer to other prejudices, this method of engaging in conversation and taking others' perspectives could be a powerful antidote to hatred and ignorance.

The Orlando massacre has left me heartbroken. The hard data further serve as a sober reminder that full LGBT equality is still in the future. However, at the same time, my ability to influence policy by voting in November and change hearts by reaching out to others gives me strength. Scientific studies such as the new one about transphobia give further hope that the hatred toward the LGBT community will erode over time.

LGBTQ People Post Both Gains and Losses in Human Rights Worldwide

Graeme Reid

Graeme Reid is the lesbian, gay, bisexual, and transgender rights director at Human Rights Watch.

Horrifying images posted on social media for all the world to see show men accused of homosexuality thrown off high buildings, stoned to death, or shot in the head by extremist groups, including the Islamic State (known as ISIS) in Iraq, Syria and Libya.

This was the worst, but by no means the only, violence directed against lesbian, gay, bisexual and transgender (LGBT) people in all parts of the world. According to a report on discrimination and violence against LGBT people by the United Nations High Commissioner for Human Rights in June:

Since 2011, hundreds of people have been killed and thousands more injured in brutal, violent attacks… Other documented violations include torture, arbitrary detention, denial of rights to assembly and expression, and discrimination in health care, education, employment and housing.

But there was also very good news for LGBT people in 2015. In May, Mexico and Ireland extended marriage to same-sex couples. A month later, Mozambique decriminalized homosexuality, and the United States Supreme Court ruled in favor of marriage equality, allowing same-sex marriages throughout the country.

Malta, Ireland, and Colombia all separated the legal process for transgender recognition from medical procedures. In June, Colombia delivered a joint statement to the UN Human Rights Council on behalf of 72 countries, from all regions of the world, affirming a commitment to end violence and discrimination based on sexual orientation and gender identity.

"Equality to Brutality: Global Trends in LGBT Rights," Graeme Reid, January 7, 2016. Reprinted by permission.

Extreme violence—and rapid progress

Extreme violence and rapid progress toward equality are the bookends of 2015. Negative snapshots include proposed draft laws that would mimic Russia's notorious "propaganda law" by setting penalties for providing objective or positive information about homosexuality in Kyrgyzstan, Kazakhstan and Belarus.

In a setback for transgender women, a Malaysian federal court reversed a ruling that had found unconstitutional a Sharia (Islamic law) provision that forbids "a male person posing as a woman," and religious authorities continued arresting trans women. In Brunei and Indonesia's Aceh province, new Sharia laws call for public lashing, imprisonment and even the death penalty for same-sex conduct. Egypt imprisoned gay men and transgender women on "debauchery" charges and Morocco routinely imprisoned men accused of homosexuality.

LGBT people in Nigeria experienced violence and abuse under the shadow of an extreme anti-LGBT law. In Gambia, home of the African Commission on Human and Peoples' Rights, gay men and lesbians fled a politically motivated crackdown. In the United States, after a campaign of fear-mongering against transgender people, voters in the city of Houston rejected a non-discrimination ordinance that would have prevented discrimination not only on the grounds of gender identity and sexual orientation, but also for race, age, and other categories.

Slovenia, in a referendum, shot down marriage equality just months after parliament extended marriage to same-sex couples.

Positive snapshots during the year include progress for transgender people in India and Thailand, where legal developments hold the promise for increased protection and social inclusion. LGBT groups in Kenya and Tunisia have been allowed to register and operate in an important assertion of the right to association. Malawi upheld a moratorium on arrests for consensual same-sex conduct, pending a court review in which activists challenged discriminatory laws. And Nepal's otherwise deeply flawed constitution includes a ray of light in a clause protecting sexual and gender minorities.

A plea for protection, and a pushback

Developments at the United Nations give insight into global trends and emerging patterns on matters relating to sexual orientation and gender identity. On September 29, at a high-level LGBT core group event at UN headquarters, Secretary-General Ban Ki-moon delivered an impassioned plea for the protection of LGBT people worldwide, and on the same day 12 UN agencies issued a joint statement on combatting violence and discrimination against LGBT and intersex people—the first of its kind.

But there is strong pushback. Russia has for years been positioning itself as the champion of "traditional values," in alliance with other countries, primarily from the Middle East and Africa. This provides a convenient positive spin for rights-abusing states to cloak crackdowns on independent groups, restrictions on the political opposition, and moves to curtail individual freedoms as upholding "traditional values."

Russian-sponsored UN resolutions on "traditional values" have attempted to undermine the universality of human rights. Russia and its allies have sought to create a false dichotomy between traditional values and human rights. And the rights of LGBT people, along with women's reproductive rights, are the lightning rods in this debate.

This dynamic played itself out in an Egypt-led resolution on the "protection of the family" that the Human Rights Council adopted in June. The resolution seeks to enshrine a narrow conception of the family as the protector of "morals" and "traditions," with no meaningful consideration of whether these comply with international human rights standards. Russia blocked attempts by South Africa, Brazil and Uruguay to recognize a broader definition of family.

Homophobia as a political tool

Such resolutions are thinly veiled attempts to use the language and institutions of human rights to push back against the rights of LGBT people, and all those who don't fit patriarchal norms. This coincides with the increased political use of homophobia, by leaders who have portrayed themselves as guardians of embattled "traditional values" to distract attention from their failures of governance.

Rhetoric that positions LGBT people as the antithesis of "morality" and "tradition" is dangerous and contributes to a hostile climate in which extreme violence occurs.

While the past year has seen significant gains, many challenges lie ahead. In countries where repressive governments attack civil society organizations and prevent them operating freely and openly, LGBT people will be forced to live a shadow existence. Civil society organizations should reject attempts by governments to manipulate anti-LGBT animus for short-term political gain, and LGBT groups should avoid working in isolation and support a broader human rights agenda.

LGBTQ People Are Not Safe in America

Douglas Quan

Douglas Quan is a reporter for the National Post, *a Canadian English-language newspaper.*

Eric Pineault says his heart sank Sunday morning when he went on Facebook and learned of a gunman's deadly assault on an Orlando, Fla., gay nightclub.

Pineault, the president of Montreal Pride, had visited the Pulse a couple years ago while on vacation. It was a smallish club with the usual top-40 tunes and thrumming house music. But like all other gay nightclubs, it was a place of comfort—where you could let your guard down.

"People can hang out and be themselves. It is not always possible to hold your lover's hand on the street. There, you can kiss and be yourself," he said. "No boundaries."

For Pineault and other activists in the LGBT community, the massacre stirred feelings not only of shock and disbelief, but also of violation. The incident also served as a stark reminder that, despite the progress that has been made to advance LGBT rights and build a culture of acceptance, community members remain targets of violence.

"That's our lived reality in terms of how LGBT people move through the world," said Helen Kennedy, executive director of Egale, which promotes LGBT rights.

"It's a reminder that it's still not safe out there and that we still are targets."

"We're still so vulnerable," said Alica Hall, co-chair of Pride Toronto, which is in the midst of celebrating the city's first Pride Month.

"'We Still Are Targets': LGBT Activists Say Orlando Shooting a Stark Reminder of Violence They Face," Douglas Quan, June 12, 2016. Material republished with the express permission of: National Post, a division of Postmedia Network Inc.

"Our progress is truly fragile."

The gunman suspected of massacring 50 people and injuring 53 others in Orlando is reported to have pledged allegiance to the Islamic State and expressed hostility toward the LGBT community.

His father, Mir Seddique (also known as Seddique Mateen), told NBC News his son once saw two men kissing each other in downtown Miami and "got very angry."

"He said, 'Look at that. In front of my son they are doing that.'"

In March, a Central Florida TV station reported that an Orlando mosque had invited a Muslim scholar with a history of condemning homosexuality to speak. The report linked to a video from a talk he gave in 2013 in which he said the punishment for homosexuality was death.

"We have to have that compassion for people. With homosexuals, it's the same," he said. "Out of compassion, let's get rid of them now."

Several Muslim organizations, including the National Council of Canadian Muslims, condemned the mass shooting.

Violence against the LGBT community around the world remains a "grave concern," said a blog post on the Amnesty International website last month.

The column cited reports of ISIL terrorists killing dozens of men in Iraq and Syria who were believed to be gay by throwing them off building rooftops; mobs beating and turning over to police members of the LGBT community in Nigeria; and extremists hacking to death two gay-rights activists in Bangladesh, including the editor of the country's only LGBT magazine.

In March, a jury in New York found Elliot Morales guilty of a hate-crime murder in the shooting death of Mark Carson in 2013. Morales reportedly unleashed a series of gay slurs at Carson and a friend in Greenwich Village before firing a single shot at Carson's head.

In 2014, Shane Matheson was sentenced to 10 years in prison for stabbing a gay man, Scott Jones, outside a New Glasgow, N.S., club that left Jones paralyzed from the waist down.

That same year, Charles Neel pleaded guilty to manslaughter and was sentenced to eight years prison for the stabbing death of Marie Lapuz in her home in New Westminster, B.C. Lapuz was the first transgender person to serve on the executive of Sher Vancouver, a group that supports LGBT South Asians.

"There is still hate," said Alan Jernigan, president of the Vancouver Pride Society. "It's one reason why organizations like ours are still around—to create safe spaces."

Data from Statistics Canada show that, in 2013, most police-reported hate crimes were non-violent, typically involving mischief, such as graffiti. However, two-thirds of cases motivated by hatred for someone's sexual orientation involved violence.

A 2015 Justice Canada report found that police data were likely to "seriously underestimate" the extent of hate crimes targeting the LGBT community because they were less likely than other victim groups to report incidents to police.

"Analysis of calls to a hotline in Toronto run by the 519 Church Street Community Centre shows that a high incidence of hate-motivated incidents directed at gays and lesbians involve physical assault," the report said. "Only a minority of incidents reported to the hotline had been reported to the police."

As Pride organizers from Vancouver to Montreal scrambled Sunday to organize vigils to mourn those killed in Orlando, they also said they planned to step up their vigilance and reach out to police to see if any security enhancements were needed at their events.

Those who were planning to attend pride events this summer should not be dissuaded, Pineault said.

"We have to still be out there and celebrate because there's so much to be done," he said. "If we become invisible, they will win."

CHAPTER 2

Does the Promotion of LGBTQ Rights Threaten the Freedom of Others?

Overview: Rights for LGBTQ Americans May Threaten Religious Freedom

Emma Green

Emma Green is a senior associate editor at the Atlantic, *where she covers politics, policy, and religion.*

Anti-discrimination statutes are coming into conflict with laws designed to preserve freedom of conscience, especially in the private sector.

Last week, the Equal Employment Opportunity Commission dropped an astounding ruling: By a 3-2 vote, it concluded that "sexual orientation is inherently a 'sex-based consideration,' and an allegation of discrimination based on sexual orientation is necessarily an allegation of sex discrimination under Title VII."

This is a big deal: The Commission's recommendations shape rulings on federal employees' workplace-discrimination claims, and its field offices deal with claims made by employees at private organizations, as well. But the ruling is also a reminder of how complicated—and unresolved—the post-*Obergefell* legal landscape is. The Supreme Court's ruling in favor of same-sex marriage at the end of June has set the country up for two new waves of discrimination claims: those made by same-sex couples and LGBT workers, and those made by religious Americans who oppose same-sex marriage. The two may seem distinct or even opposed, but they're actually intertwined: In certain cases, extending new rights to LBGT workers will necessarily lead to religious-freedom objections, and vice versa.

Right now, it's impossible to know how these claims will fall out. It's been less than a month since the ruling, and much of the legal theory on these issues is just that: theory. In Congress, there's at least some effort to reconcile the two sides. As my colleague Russell Berman wrote on Friday, Democrats are pushing for legislation which would include prohibitions on discrimination in education, housing, and public accommodation, and Republicans may well sign on—if that legislation allows for religious exemptions. No matter what passes, the issues will remain tangled. These will be some of the questions courts and legislatures have to untangle in the wake of *Obergefell*.

Workplace and Hiring Discrimination

Many Americans may assume the Supreme Court's decision in *Obergefell* will have a direct bearing on cases of discrimination on the basis of sexual orientation. That's not quite right, said Andrew Koppelman, a law professor at Northwestern University. "The question of how you treat discrimination against gay people is just a different question [than] whether you allow them to marry," he said. "Allowing them to marry is a question of what the state does. The other question is a question of how you regulate private actors and for what reason."

A 2014 survey found that roughly 75 percent of Americans believed that federal law prohibits firing or refusing to hire someone on the basis of sexual orientation. Roughly 75 percent of Americans were wrong. Despite repeated attempts to pass the Employment Non-Discrimination Act and similar pieces of legislation in Congress, no federal protection has ever been put in place. As my colleague Joe Pinsker wrote in *The Atlantic* on Wednesday, the recent EEOC decision is an important first step toward creating these protections at the federal level, but lower courts could dispute the Commission's interpretation of Title VII. The final interpretation of this statute would have to come from the Supreme Court, particularly if lower courts challenge the Commission's decision.

Twenty-two states and the District of Columbia have laws covering sexual-orientation discrimination in areas like housing and employment, which means 28 states don't have them. Last March, Utah passed a law prohibiting sexual-orientation-based discrimination, but with an important caveat: All religious organizations, including colleges, charities, and some miscellaneous organizations like the Boy Scouts are exempt.

Which leaves an open question: What about private employers who claim to have a religious objection to having gay employees? Douglas Laycock, a law professor at the University of Virginia, was skeptical that these kinds of claims could make it very far in court—or that they'd even come up that often. "When you say, I can't have any gay person working in my [business], and it's against my religion, judges are going to be skeptical that that's a religious belief," he said. "Non-discrimination laws serve a compelling interest."

For now, the bigger issue is the ambiguity. In the absence of explicit federal protections—and in many places, state protections—someone who believed he or she was being discriminated against on the basis of sexual orientation would be totally dependent on the interpretation of the courts.

Spousal Benefits

Where things get trickier, though, is with spousal benefits. To help explain why, a bit of background: Often, when people sue for religious exemptions to certain laws, they do it under the auspices of the Religious Freedom Restoration Act, or RFRA. This June, before the same-sex-marriage ruling, the ACLU ran an op-ed in *The Washington Post* declaring that it could no longer support the federal version of RFRA. The reason it cited was the Supreme Court's decision in *Hobby Lobby*, in which the Court ruled that most private businesses could legitimately claim a religious objection to covering certain kinds of birth control in their employees' health-insurance plans, something that's now required by the Affordable Care act. "The RFRA wasn't meant to force employees to pay a price for their employer's faith," the op-ed's author, Louise Melling, wrote. "Efforts of this nature will likely only increase should the

Supreme Court rule—as is expected—that same-sex couples have the freedom to marry."

This may certainly be a symbolic political play on the part of the ACLU—just as political organizations on the right have drummed up fears about religious discrimination, so political organizations on the left have drummed up fears about LGBT discrimination. But now that the Supreme Court has set a precedent for private businesses to push for religious exemptions, it's possible that business owners will make these claims with regards to laws like the Family and Medical Leave Act, a federal statute which guarantees employees the right to unpaid leave and continued health-insurance coverage in the case of certain family or medical emergencies.

"I do anticipate the kinds of claims," said Douglas NeJaime, a law professor at UCLA. "The kind of claim that you saw in *Hobby Lobby*—you could see similar kinds of claims in the same-sex marriage context: The employer objects to providing benefits to the same-sex spouse, claiming that it makes the employer complicit in the sinful conduct it objects to."

Most of these claims would probably be brought under state versions of the Religious Freedom Restoration Act, rather than the federal version. This is because the federal version of RFRA only applies to federal laws, and as I wrote above, most anti-discrimination laws exist only at the state level.

But if you compare the states that have their own version of RFRA and those that have sexual-orientation discrimination laws, "it's like the inverse map almost," said NeJaime. "A lot of the states that don't have sexual-orientation anti-discrimination laws also have RFRAs. Everyone makes a lot of the religious-liberty claim, but in some states, there isn't even an obligation to serve gay people equally."

Where things get more interesting, he said, is at the local level. Some cities and counties in states without sexual-orientation-discrimination protections have their own ordinances that prohibit such discrimination—this includes places like Little Rock, Arkansas, and Nashville, Tennessee. If that state also had a version of RFRA on the books—as, for example, Arkansas and Tennessee both do—an employer could plausibly claim that his or her religious beliefs were being violated by the requirement to provide benefits to employees in a same-sex marriage.

Providing Goods and Services for Same-Sex Functions

Photographers, florists, and bakers all have two things in common: They all get mad business from weddings, and they all have colleagues who have refused to provide services at a same-sex marriage ceremony because of religious objections. A number of cases over the past several years have asked whether these private business owners should be required by law to serve at these weddings, and some courts have definitively answered: Yes. The husband-and-wife duo who owned Sweet Cakes bakery in Oregon was fined $135,000 this summer for turning away a lesbian couple. The New Mexico Supreme Court found last spring that the couple who owned Elane Photography violated the state's public-accommodations law when they refused to photograph a commitment ceremony between two lesbian partners. Another baker case is currently pending appeal in Colorado.

The geographic pattern of these disputes has been interesting—even though people in the South are most strongly opposed to gay marriage and partnerships, many of these religious-freedom claims have taken place outside of the South. But that's precisely because most Southern states don't have sexual-orientation-anti-discrimination laws. As NeJaime put it, "The gay person who gets turned away in Oregon can go to his lawyer and do something. The gay person who get turned away in Alabama just goes to his friends and complains."

There have been a few claims popping up elsewhere, outside of the context of weddings. In June, a Maryland DJ refused to work at the birthday party of a gay man, and in April, a Kentucky court upheld the religious-freedom claim of Hands on Originals, a T-shirt company that refused to print shirts for a gay-pride parade.

NeJaime said that there's an important distinction here, though: At least in the T-shirt case, the court ruled the claim was an issue of free speech, rather than discrimination. "It's the difference between not providing service because the person's gay and not doing something in particular because it's particular speech," he said.

Gay Adoption

Even before the Supreme Court decision, many gay couples could already adopt children. Different states have different guidelines: Some allow non-biological parents to adopt only within the context of marriage. Others allow gay partners to adopt their partner's child even if the couple isn't married, which is called a second-parent adoption. "The big distinction after *Obergefell* is really about marital status rather than sexual orientation," NeJaime said.

But there may be complications coming. In June, Michigan passed a law allowing religious adoption agencies to turn down prospective parents whose lifestyles don't accord with their religious beliefs, including gay or unmarried couples. Florida considered a similar measure this spring, although that bill died in the senate in May. This was one of the religious-freedom concerns John Roberts specifically called out in his dissent to the Court's decision in *Obergefell*.

The other consideration, NeJaime said, is healthcare-refusal laws: "In every state, there are laws that allow people to refuse to provide services in healthcare based on a religious or moral objection." Most of these have to do with abortion, he said, but some now include provisions about assisted reproductive technologies, like artificial insemination, which could potentially have a big effect on lesbian couples who are trying to get pregnant.

Issuing Same-Sex Marriage Licenses and Performing Wedding Ceremonies

As the possibility of legal, nationwide gay marriage loomed nearer this summer, many politicians voiced their concern for the religious freedom of clerks, judges, and clergy members who didn't want to issue same-sex marriage licenses or perform ceremonies. North Carolina, for example, passed a law in advance of the ruling stating that any judge who doesn't want to perform same-sex-marriage ceremonies can choose not to perform marriages of any kind for a period of six months.

Now that the ruling has passed, several cases like this have already come up. For example, Kim Davis, the clerk of Rowan County, Kentucky, is being sued for refusing to issue marriage licenses to gay couples. And Joyce Lewis-Kugle, the clerk of Rusk County, Texas, resigned a few weeks after the Supreme Court's decision because, she said, "the laws I swore to protect have changed." Any clerk or judge who makes this kind of claim may face litigation, but they'll also have ample resources to defend themselves—as Texas Attorney General Ken Paxton announced after the ruling, "numerous lawyers stand ready to assist clerks defending their religious beliefs."

The legal facts are a bit different for clergy, though. After the ruling, several states, including Texas and Tennessee, put together "pastor protection acts," allegedly to ensure that pastors wouldn't have to perform gay marriages if those unions violate their religious beliefs.

"The pastor protection acts are purely symbolic politics for the following reason: The government cannot discriminate ... when recognizing marriage, but certainly my rabbi can," said Mark Graber, a law professor at the University of Maryland. "My rabbi had that right before *Obergefell*, and my rabbi has that right afterwards. My rabbi, by the First Amendment, only has to perform religious marriages that my rabbi believes are sanctified by Jewish law."

Sexual-Conduct Policies at Religious Universities

One final arena to keep an eye on is that of religious colleges and universities. Some leaders at Christian schools, including many that identify as evangelical, fear they may be stripped of their tax-exempt status, lose their access to federal funding, or face other problems because of their policies on homosexuality. There haven't been many instances of this in action yet—the most prominent example is that of Gordon College, which faced the possible loss of its accreditation from the New England Association of Schools and Colleges in 2014 because of its ban on "homosexual practice." After nearly a year of internal review, the school announced it would keep its sexual-conduct guidelines … and nothing happened. But other issues, like whether these schools must provide equal housing accommodations to straight and gay married couples, may arise.

LGBTQ Rights Threaten Some Americans

David Elcott

David Elcott is Taub Professor of Practice in Public Service and Leadership at the Robert F. Wagner Graduate School of Public Service at New York University.

T he Supreme Court decision to legalize same-sex marriage drew such a strong reaction from every side that it seemed to reflect that Americans live in a country riven by irreconcilable theological values.

In arguing for the majority, Justice Anthony Kennedy contended that same-sex marriage was in harmony with the highest ideals of religion: love, fidelity, devotion, sacrifice, family and dignity.

To the court's detractors, however, the ruling turned Bible teachings on their head. "Today the Court is wrong again," the US Conference of Catholic Bishops stated. "It is profoundly immoral and unjust for the government to declare that two people of the same sex can constitute a marriage."

Pockets of resistance have kept the issue in the news. Best-known is Kim Davis, the Kentucky clerk who was jailed after refusing to issue marriage licenses to same-sex couples, citing religious objections. Other clerks have voiced similar objections.

This is not simply another political debate over what policies are best suited for Americans. Instead, it is part of a long-running battle over what God wants of American Christians. As such, compromise will not be possible until the combatants discern the religious underpinnings that motivate and guide their political adversaries.

As an advocate of reconciliation, I have spent years engaged in interfaith and interethnic work. So I recently set off from my

"Why Some Religious Americans See Same-Sex Marriage as a Threat," David Elcott, The Conversation, October 12, 2015. https://theconversation.com/why-some-religious -americans-see-same-sex-marriage-as-a-threat-48008. Licensed under CC BY ND 4.0 International.

home in New York City, looking for the seeds of a more productive national discourse on same-sex marriage.

With my research team, we visited a dozen Christian churches of different denominations, from Georgia Pentecostals to liberals in New England. I chose churches from a variety of regions, whose members had different levels of wealth and a variety of racial makeups. I cannot name the churches because I promised anonymity to those interviewed.

A shared interest in public policy

As different as the congregations were, they had one thing in common—they all engaged in public policy issues as one aspect of their religious calling, translating the values they hold dear into beliefs about how American society should function.

That religion helps shape the culture of which it is a part should seem cliched. A healthy society will meaningfully address core values if it is to flourish. Researchers like Jonathan Haidt and others who study how cultures evolve, argue that all societies share values such as compassion, fairness, respect for authority and loyalty.

In visiting churches, our goal was to test how these values are expressed and translated into public policy. Although we conducted surveys that probed many of these values, for conservatives one question seemed to trump the others—a concern about purity and pollution.

All societies—religious or secular—have an idea about what is pure or sacred, and attempt to protect the pure. This is not just about religion. Cultures may be unique, but they all teach human beings, whether religious or not, to respond to what their society considers sacred. In some places, dogs were considered deities; in others, dirty. To burn the flag can be seen as an ugly defilement—or a sign of a vital democracy.

In the Hebrew Bible, certain diseases, menstrual blood and pigs are examples of pollution. Many Christians also turn to the Bible to ground their understanding of the pure and impure. For conservative Christians, sex can be the great defiler and challenge to God.

This may lead one to expect that conservative Christians would exhibit severe homophobia and hatred against those whose sexual practices and beliefs diverged from their own. There certainly is homophobia in America . Yet in my conversations with congregants of every denomination, homophobia wasn't much in evidence.

Instead, what emerged in our conversations was a central shared belief that we are all sinners, we have no right to distinguish one sin from another, and God wants all of us to repent.

As a minister in Georgia said to me, "If I were to shut my doors to my brother for being gay, then what does that say about the church and Jesus's message?"

In Kentucky, I heard: "We teach that you could be clear in what you teach [about] same-sex marriage, and also teach that those people are beloved of God and should be welcomed."

So if it is not homophobia, what is at the core of such anger and pain over same-sex marriage?

A clarifying question

Digging deeper into the mindsets of the religious Americans we surveyed, I found a clear distinction in the ways conservative and liberal Christians see the world. This distinction was highlighted by a specific question we asked churchgoers and clergy:

Though you may believe in both, which better reflects your views:

1. The world is primarily a dangerous place filled with the potential for sinful and evil forces.

2. The world is primarily filled with the potential for goodness, care, and cooperation.

Those who chose the first response, that the world is dangerous with sin and evil, held consistently negative views on everything from same-sex marriage to premarital sex, abortion and condoms for minors.

Those who believed the world is filled with goodness, care and cooperation chose the opposite responses on each of the issues.

To the Christian population that sees the world filled with sin and evil, same-sex marriage represents a pollution. It undermines the core of what is sacred and holy. And the sin, the pollution, is not limited to the sinners alone.

As my father-in-law, the noted biblical scholar Jacob Milgrom, explains, evildoers "[b]ring down the righteous with them. Those who perish with the wicked are not entirely blameless, however. They are inadvertent sinners who, by having allowed the wicked to flourish, have also contributed to the pollution of the sanctuary."

For Christian believers in the United States, such pollution threatens to overwhelm the society of which they are a part and undermine its moral fiber. Same-sex marriage wreaks havoc on the core belief that America can be a fulfillment of biblical prophecy and moral rectitude.

However, this was not the case for the great majority of mainstream Christians we surveyed and interviewed. Their focus was on compassion and fairness, as theologian Katherine Henderson declared:

> "As people of faith, we believe that every human being is created in the image of God and has sacred worth. Laws that grant rights and protections to some but not to others, simply because of gender or sexual orientation, are moral outrages."

Our survey showed conservative congregants experienced their opposition to same-sex marriage as a desire to make whole something they see as ruptured that endangers all of us. Mainstream Christians saw same-sex marriage as an expression of divine love and justice. Interviews and focus groups confirmed these two core responses to same-sex marriage extended to the other questions, such as distributing condoms in schools and premarital sex in general.

Hope for the future

I came away from my recent journey with a much better appreciation for the coherent, theologically based value systems that fuel bitter red state/blue state divisions. Yet, I also saw opportunity for understanding and reconciliation.

Same-sex marriage is here to stay—America does not take away rights and privileges. And while I do not anticipate seeing two men kneeling at their own Catholic church wedding any time soon, there is ample evidence that while purity values are a constant, the object of "contamination" changes over times.

As gay and lesbian couples marry, have children, send them to school, attend church, participate in the civic, social and business life of the community, and are out as members of our own families, homosexuality may well cease to trigger the types of negative responses seen today.

As one congregant in Georgia noted, her now multiethnic church once preached segregation. Perhaps, she mused, her grandchildren will view church views on homosexuality with equal disappointment.

LGBTQ Rights Threaten Businesses

Kristine Marsh

Kristine Marsh is an analyst for the Media Research Center's News Analysis Division. The Media Research Center is a conservative media watchdog organization whose mission is to counteract a liberal bias in the news media.

E ven though gay marriage advocates often say those marriages won't hurt others, business owners have been finding out that isn't true. Companies, especially wedding-related ones, from several states have been sued and harassed for holding onto religious convictions.

The concept of "gay rights" has trampled religious liberty, but the network news media haven't noticed. In fact, when Family Research Council's Tony Perkins was on CBS in June, Bob Schieffer said he was "unaware" of such cases. In a year of coverage about discrimination cases involving gays, there was only casual mention of an attack on businesses out of 31 stories on the network news broadcasts (Nov. 1, 2012 through Oct. 31, 2013). And that was a casual comment about Chick-Fil-A. Even after additional searches for coverage of specific lawsuits, the broadcast networks have said almost nothing in recent years about the impact of gay rights and gay marriage on businesses.

The situation for businesses and Christian business owners could worsen if Congress passes the Employee Non-Discrimination Act (ENDA). The legislation "would outlaw workplace discrimination based on sexual orientation and gender identity," according to The New York Times. House Speaker John Boehner announced

"Gay Rights Movement's Threatens Businesses," Kristine Marsh, MRC Research Center (mrc.org), May 11, 2013. Reprinted with permission.

his opposition to the bill on Nov. 4, and the bill is not expected to be able to pass the House, according to The Washington Post.

Several states including New Mexico, Oregon, Illinois, Washington and Iowa each have their own state's "Human Rights Act" or "Civil Rights Act" which prohibit discrimination by public businesses based on sexual orientation.

The wedding industry been hardest hit by the tension between religious liberty and gay rights, in spite of a recent Rasmussen poll showing that 85% of Americans think business owners should be allowed to deny services for gay weddings if they have religious objections. Other companies like Chick-Fil-A and Barilla Pasta have been targeted as well for making statements that angered gay activists.

In 2006, Elaine Huguenin, a Christian photographer in New Mexico, declined a request to photograph a "commitment ceremony" and was subsequently taken to court. She defended her religious rights but was ruled against by the New Mexico Supreme Court in August 2013. She was ordered to pay more than $6,000 in legal fees. In a concurring opinion on the case, one justice even stated that having to violate your religious beliefs when they conflict with social issues like gay marriage "is the price of citizenship." The photographer and her attorneys are considering taking the case to the U.S. Supreme Court.

The ACLU and the Colorado attorney general are suing the owner of Masterpiece Cakeshop, a Colorado bakery, according to The Blaze. The owner is facing up to a year in jail time for refusing to bake a gay couple a wedding cake in 2012. The ACLU echoed the sentiment of the New Mexico court justice saying, "But someone's personal religious beliefs don't justify breaking the law by discriminating against others in the public sphere."

ABC News.com reported that a Washington florist was sued in April by the state's attorney general on behalf of a same-sex couple who were declined flowers for their wedding ceremony. The couple who sued the florist were regular customers of the florist for 10 years, but when the florist was asked to provide flowers for a same-sex wedding, she told CBN, that she "had to take a stand."

The florist is now counter-suing with the help of the Alliance Defending Freedom. The Washington Attorney General stated, "As an individual, she is free to hold religious beliefs but as a business owner, she may not violate our state's laws against discrimination— no matter what she personally believes."

Networks Barely Mention Harm to Businesses

ABC, CBS and NBC news programs have barely addressed the stories of business owners accused of anti-gay discrimination, or the ensuing harassment and lawsuits.

Apart from a few local news stories, the bulk of these reports have come from conservative and religious blogs and far left and gay websites. The liberal websites predictably attacked businesses for being "homophobic." The Huffington Post even has "anti-gay companies list," which includes chains like Chic-Fil-A, Domino's Pizza, and Exxon but also charities like the Salvation Army.

CBS' Bob Schieffer claimed to be "unaware" of any of these lawsuits in a June 30 interview with the Family Research Council's Tony Perkins.

After Perkins cited cases in Washington, New Mexico and Colorado, where the state's anti-discrimination statutes were being forced on religious business owners, Schieffer said, "This is under my radar, I haven't—I haven't heard this."

Perkins then pointed out the failure of the media to cover the topic saying, "Well, you know, Bob, that`s a great point, because the media's not reporting on this because they realize there's a lot more behind this than the marriage altar. It's literally about altering the landscape of America."

While Schieffer plead ignorance, ABC found a way to spin the issue sympathetically for gay couples. In a July 13 episode of "What Would You Do?" ABC set up a fake bakery that denied services to actors portraying lesbians in front of unsuspecting strangers. This episode clearly was a mock-up of the real case of

Christian-owned Oregon bakery Sweet Cakes by Melissa. A lesbian couple sued the bakery for refusing to bake their wedding cake for religious reasons.

ABC chose not to report the real story. Sweet Cakes by Melissa shutdown after a "vicious boycott" along with obscene hate mail and death threats from LGBT community. Aaron Klein, owner of Sweet Cakes told Fox News' Todd Starnes: "The LGBT attacks are the reason we are shutting down the shop. They have killed our business through mob tactics."

Multiple wedding venues have been harassed as well. Owners of a venue in Iowa received angry emails, phone calls and death threats and are currently facing a lawsuit for refusing to let a gay couple use their venue to get married, according to The Blaze. There have been similar stories in Texas, and Vermont, according to a local NBC affiliate and TownHall.

The left has cheered on these lawsuits. Slate writer Mark Joseph Stern said in an article that argued discrimination is not "religious liberty": "But when a state bans private discrimination against gay people, there's always a losing side—the homophobes. And even if these homophobes' cause is bigoted, their seemingly principled stand in the name of religious liberty can evoke more sympathy than NOM's shrill shrieks."

And it isn't just the wedding business.

A Christian T-shirt company was sued against in 2012 for refusing to print shirts for a LGBT gay pride festival in Kentucky. The courts sided with the gay rights group in the end.

Recently, when Guido Barilla of Barilla Pasta Company said he would not feature gay families in his company's advertisements, gay rights activists in Italy launched a boycott but the backlash spread beyond Italy's borders. The comment sparked social media attacks.

His simple statement that "sacred family remains one of the basic values of the company" made in an Italian radio interview was intolerable according to activists. Barilla has issued multiple apologies but it hasn't been enough to pacify the left.

An account called "Boycott Barilla" posted this tweet on October 21: "Even the Pope is more liberal than homophobic #Barilla!" Gay actor George Takei also took to Twitter to bash Barilla with "I hear Barilla pasta is making a new product— bigotoni." Harvard University even went so far as to stop serving the brand in their dining halls. The Huffington Post ran the story, "12 Pasta Brands That Haven't Pissed Off Gay People."

Business Owners Cannot Use Religion to Discriminate

Zack Ford

Zack Ford is LGBT editor at ThinkProgress, a progressive news site associated with the Center for American Progress Action Fund.

I n July of 2012, the Masterpiece Cakeshop in Colorado refused to sell a wedding cake to a same-sex couple who were planning to celebrate with friends and family the marriage they had received in Massachusetts. The couple, Dave Mullins and Charlie Craig, filed a complaint, and the Colorado Attorney General proceeded to do the same, and Friday, Administrative Law Judge (ALJ) Robert Spencer ruled against Jack Phillips, the owner of the bakery.

Here are some of the arguments from ADJ Spencer's ruling as to why "religious freedom" did not justify Phillips' violation of Colorado's nondiscrimination law protecting sexual orientation:

It Doesn't Matter If The Bakery Otherwise Serves Gay People

One of the bakery's arguments was that it still served gay clients—the owner only objected to a wedding cake that would celebrate a same-sex marriage. Spencer argued that since only gay couples would participate in same-sex marriage, it's a "distinction without a difference."

Respondents deny that they hold any animus toward homosexuals or gay couples, and would willingly provide other types of baked goods to Complainants or any other gay customer. On the other hand, Respondents would refuse to provide a wedding cake to a heterosexual customer if it was for a same-sex wedding.

The ALJ rejects Respondents' argument as a distinction without a difference.

The salient feature distinguishing same-sex weddings from heterosexual ones is the sexual orientation of its participants. Only same-sex couples engage in same-sex weddings. Therefore, it makes little sense to argue that refusal to provide a cake to a same-sex couple for use at their wedding is not "because of" their sexual orientation.

This Case Has Nothing To Do With Whether Same-Sex Marriage Is Legal

Conservatives often argue that cases like these that allegedly impose on "religious liberty" are the consequence of marriage equality passing, but Colorado doesn't have marriage equality. The judge notes that this actually proves that the discrimination is based on the couple's identity:

Nor is the ALJ persuaded by Respondents' argument that they should be compelled to recognize same-sex marriages because Colorado does not do so. Although Respondents are correct that Colorado does not recognize same-sex marriage, that fact does not excuse discrimination based upon sexual orientation. At oral argument, Respondents candidly acknowledged that they would also refuse to provide a cake to a same-sex couple for a commitment ceremony or a civil union, neither of which is forbidden by Colorado law. Because Respondents' objection goes beyond just the act of "marriage," and extends to any union of a same-sex couple, it is apparent that Respondents' real objection is to the couple's sexual orientation and not simply their marriage.

Cakes Do Not Constitute "Speech"

Though the judge was sympathetic that cakes require artistry, he dismissed the idea that they constituted speech. In this case, the bakery refused to provide the cake before the couple could even specify what would or would not be on the cake, thus there is not even any speech to consider:

The ALJ, however, rejects Respondents' argument that preparing a wedding cake is necessarily a medium of expression amounting to protected "speech," or that compelling Respondents to treat same-sex and heterosexual couples equally is the equivalent of forcing Respondents to adhere to "an ideological point of view." There is no doubt that decorating a wedding cake involves considerable skill and artistry. However, the finished product does not necessarily qualify as "speech," as would saluting a flag, marching in a parade, or displaying a motto.

The undisputed evidence is that Phillips categorically refused to prepare a cake for Complainants' same-sex wedding before there was any discussion about what the cake would look like. Phillips was not asked to apply any message or symbol to the cake, or to construct the cake in any fashion that could be reasonably understood as advocating same-sex marriage. After being refused, Complainants immediately left the shop. For all Phillips knew at the time, Complainants might have wanted a nondescript cake that would have been suitable for consumption at any wedding. Therefore, Respondents' claim that they refused to provide a cake because it would convey a message supporting same-sex marriage is specious. The act of preparing a cake is simply not "speech" warranting First Amendment protection.

In a footnote, the judge notes that the couple did eventually obtain a cake that had "a filling with rainbow colors," but expressed doubt that it would have justified Phillips' "categorical refusal" to bake a cake for them.

The Act Of Selling Cakes Also Does Not Constitute "Speech"

Regardless of what the cake itself might communicate or not, the act of selling cakes is also not a form of speech; thus, forcing a bakery to sell to a same-sex couple is not compelled speech:

Compelling a bakery that sells wedding cakes to heterosexual couples to also sell wedding cakes to same-sex couples is incidental to the state's right to prohibit discrimination on the basis of sexual orientation, and is not the same as forcing a person to pledge allegiance to the government or to display a motto with which they disagree. To say otherwise trivializes the right to free speech.

Spencer went on to dismiss other offensive hypothetical situations, noting that they don't apply since a cake was refused based on identity, not on content:

Respondents argue that if they are compelled to make a cake for a same-sex wedding, then a black baker could not refuse to make a cake bearing a white-supremacist message for a member of the Aryan Nation; and an Islamic baker could not refuse to make a cake denigrating the Koran for the Westboro Baptist Church. However, neither of these fanciful hypothetical situations proves Respondents' point. In both cases, it is the explicit, unmistakable, offensive message that the bakers are asked to put on the cake that gives rise to the bakers' free speech right to refuse. That, however, is not the case here, where Respodnents refused to bake any cake for Complainants regardless of what was written on it or what it looked like. Respondents have no free speech right to refuse because they were only asked to bake a cake, not make a speech.

Baking Cakes Is Not Religious Conduct

Though Phillips objected to providing the cake on religious grounds, the ALJ pointed out that baking a cake is not actually conduct that is part of his religion. Thus, it does not qualify for exemption from regulation:

Respondents' refusal to provide a cake for Complainants' same-sex wedding is distinctly the type of conduct that the Supreme Court has repeatedly found subject to legitimate regulation. Such discrimination is against the law; it adversely affects the rights of Complainants to be free from discrimination in the marketplace; and the impact upon Respondents is incidental to the state's legitimate regulation of commercial activity. Respondents therefore have no valid claim that barring them from discriminating against same-sex customers violates their right to free exercise of religion. Conceptually, Respondents' refusal to serve a same-sex couple due to religious objection to same-sex weddings is no different from refusing to serve a biracial couple because of religious objection to biracial marriage. However, that argument was struck down long ago in *Bob Jones Univ. v. United States*.

This case could have implications for similar cases playing out in other states, such as another bakery in Oregon, a florist in Washington, and a photographer in New Mexico, whose case has now been appealed to the U.S. Supreme Court.

Tolerance Is Needed to Protect LGBTQ Rights and Religious Freedoms

Cody Cain

Cody Cain is a writer and commentator living in New York City.

Gay marriage has just been legalized all across the nation by the United States Supreme Court in the landmark ruling, *Obergefell v. Hodges.*

Left wing liberals are jumping for joy. Right wing religious conservatives are horrified. So where does this leave us as a people? Well, let's see if we can sort through some of the fall-out.

First and foremost, it is important to emphasize that religious conservatives need not be alarmed by this decision because your views remain fully protected by our Constitution. Many of you believe that marriage can be legitimate only if between one man and one woman. This view was articulated by the Texas Republican Governor Greg Abbott when he said that "marriage was defined by God," and "no man can redefine it."

Many of you also believe that gay marriage is morally wrong. This view was expressed by Archbishop Joseph Kurtz of Louisville, Kentucky, president of the U.S. Conference of Catholic Bishops, when he said that the notion is "profoundly immoral and unjust" that "two people of the same sex can constitute a marriage."

Don't worry, this case did not change any of that and thus you are still perfectly free to hold these beliefs. In fact, the majority opinion in this case directly addressed this very point in resounding language: "Finally, it must be emphasized that religions, and those who adhere to religious doctrines, may continue to advocate with utmost, sincere conviction that, by divine precepts, same-sex marriage should not be condoned."

"Religious Freedom vs. Gay Rights: Can We All Get Along?" Cody Cain, July 6, 2015. Reprinted with permission.

Wow. That's powerful stuff.

The Court went on to say very clearly that your right to your religious beliefs and your traditional way of life are expressly protected by our Constitution: "The First Amendment ensures that religious organizations and persons are given proper protection as they seek to teach the principles [of traditional marriage] that are so fulfilling and so central to their lives and faiths, and to their own deep aspirations to continue the [traditional] family structure they have long revered."

This language should be deeply comforting to religious conservatives as it reaffirms that your beliefs of being opposed to gay marriage are indeed fully protected. Phew! Religious conservatives can breathe a sigh of relief. You are not under attack, there is no threat to your beliefs or your way of life, and thus there is no need for you to take up arms and charge into battle.

What the Court did here was merely to say that these profound rights enshrined in our Constitution to believe as you wish and to conduct your way of life in accordance with your beliefs apply not only to religious conservatives, but these rights apply to other people as well. The ruling simply stands for the proposition that if you happen to be opposed to gay marriage, that's perfectly fine, and if you happen to be in favor of gay marriage, that's perfectly fine too. It's up to you. This, in fact, is the essence of what religious freedom is all about (though the Court's ruling was based upon the fundamental right of marriage as opposed to freedom of religion). At the end of the day, the effect of the legal aspect of the ruling is simply that the government cannot outlaw either type of marriage.

So what does this mean for people living in the real world out in society? Can we all get along with each other if we have different beliefs?

Hm. Let's see here. Well, the freedom of religion enshrined in our Constitution already gives us the framework for getting along despite having religious differences. The key is simply to honor the principle that it must be a two-way street. The first part of the two-way street is easy for everyone. Our own beliefs are protected and others cannot impose their beliefs upon us. We all agree with that one. But the second part is less easy for some people. The second part is that, by the same token, we must reciprocate by not seeking to impose our beliefs upon others.

Uh oh. That's the hard part. It is this second part that is difficult for some people and we already see people struggling with it, mainly religious conservatives. These folks are fine with the first part of the two-way street, and the first part for them is not under challenge at all as no one is seeking to require religious conservatives to marry people of their own gender against their will. No, of course not. Nor is anyone seeking to prevent these religious conservatives from marrying traditionally as they please. No, of course not. These religious conservatives are entirely free to practice their own beliefs and there is no threat whatsoever of taking away any of their rights to do so.

But some of these religious conservatives find it very difficult to abide by the second part of the two-way street of reciprocating to others. They are not content to allow others to practice beliefs that differ from their own. Instead, these religious conservatives seek to impose their own beliefs upon others by preventing others from consummating gay marriages. It is this second part of the two-way street that is causing all the trouble.

We see this manifested in various ways, such as when local officials cite their religious beliefs and refuse to issue marriage licenses to gay couples. The rights of these officials are not in any way in jeopardy as they are free to marry traditionally as they choose, but yet they deny the rights of other people to marry when these other people happen to have different beliefs. Withholding marriage licenses is obviously outrageous as we would never stand for this if officials refused to issue marriage licenses on other religious grounds, such as to interfaith couples, interracial couples, or couples with out-of-wedlock children.

We have also seen this problem when businesses refuse to serve gay customers, such as the pizza parlor that refused to serve pizza to gay people, florists that have refused to provide flowers for gay weddings, and bakeries that have refused to make wedding cakes for gay marriages. We have seen it in the so called "religious freedom" laws as well, which should be named more accurately "religious imposition" laws. The initial federal religious freedom law was conceived with the good intention of protecting people with minority religious beliefs, namely Native Americans, but then this law was shrewdly twisted into laws designed to permit people of the majority religion (conservative Christians) to discriminate against people with different views (gay people).

These are all examples of failing to honor the second part of the two-way street. The people who deny services are not at risk themselves of having their own beliefs taken away in any manner. They are free to practice their own beliefs as they desire. But they are opposed to the beliefs of other people, so they seek to deny goods and services to these other people who happen to have different beliefs.

Such denial of service to people who do not share the religious belief system of the majority is entirely inconsistent with the fundamental principal of freedom of religion. The whole point of freedom of religion is that people should be free to believe whatever they wish, even if their beliefs are different from the majority, and they should not suffer discrimination as a result of their minority views. Delivering flowers to a gay person, or serving pizza to a gay person, does not make you gay. It also does not mean that you condone being gay in any way.

Denying service represents a breakdown of the two-way street of respecting the rights of others, and indeed a breakdown of our free and fair society. Just think what would happen if we moved away from the freedom of religion contemplated in our Constitution and instead toward a system of these so-called "religious freedom" laws that allow religious observers to deny service to anyone based upon their own religious beliefs. We would have chaos. We already have local officials denying marriage licenses, some denying marriage licenses to both straight and gay couples, which is a clear example of the breakdown of the functions of the state.

But multiply this exponentially if it were adopted throughout society. Mail carriers could skip delivering mail to people they suspected of holding impure beliefs. State officials could deny issuing driver's licenses. Insurance companies could deny insurance. Landlords could deny housing. Hospitals could deny care. Restaurants could deny diners. Schools could deny students. Check-out clerks could refuse to check people out.

And it is not just gay people who could be denied service, but it could be anyone deemed unsatisfactory by the particular religious observer, such as anyone who has not been baptized, who fails to dress in a certain way, or who eats pork.

Where would it end?

It is, of course, ridiculous. This is not who we are as Americans.

So given all of our differences, can we all get along?

Yes, we can all get along. Even if some people are gay, and even if some of these gay people are married, we can still all get along. The framework is already in place under the principles of freedom of religion in our own Constitution. Freedom of religion is a cornerstone of what makes America great and what enables us to all get along despite our very different beliefs. We just need to be mindful that it is a two-way street. All we need is just a small amount of religious tolerance to refrain from imposing our own beliefs upon others, and to allow others to practice their own beliefs freely.

It's really not very much to ask.

CHAPTER 3

Is Same-Sex Marriage a Human Right?

Overview: Same-Sex Marriage Highlights Tension over Fundamental Rights

Danaya Wright

Danaya Wright is a professor of law at the University of Florida.

The Supreme Court's decision in *Obergefell v Hodges* fulfilled predictions that the court would affirm marriage equality nationwide as a fundamental constitutional right.

However, the case also offered a few surprises and a few disappointments.

To understand those, one needs to put the decision into its historical and legal frameworks.

From sacrament to contract

For centuries of Western history, the question of who controls the legal aspects of marriage has been highly contested.

Until the 16th century, the Catholic Church defined the conditions for marriage. Since the Reformation, there has been a continuous debate between ecclesiastical authorities and civil authorities about issues including who can marry and what rights and responsibilities marriage confers.

Over time, however, marriage shifted from being a sacrament to a civil contract as governments took the power to define marriage from religious sources.

In the United States, it was the legislature within each state that defined the criteria for entry into marriage by prohibiting some pairings, such as interracial marriages and marriages between minors, and imposing blood tests and registration requirements.

"The Surprises in the Supreme Court's Same-Sex Marriage Decision," Danaya Wright, The Conversation, June 30, 2015. https://theconversation.com/the-surprises-in-the-supreme -courts-same-sex-marriage-decision-43684. Licensed under CC BY ND 4.0 International.

Marriage in the United States has always been a civil contract entered into between the two parties and the state and, although it can be performed by religious authorities, its validity is determined by reference to civil law.

This arrangement is mandated by the constitutional prohibition against an established religion and is the result of this country being governed by a secular legal system.

Until the late 20th century, the question of same-sex marriages wasn't even up for debate because same-sex relationships were criminalized in most states.

Requesting a marriage license, in other words, was tantamount to confessing to a crime.

Gay rights and equal protection

As the gay rights movement began to flourish in the years after the Stonewall riots of 1969, states started decriminalizing same-sex intimate relations. And as that happened, gay couples sought greater and greater legal protections against discrimination.

Most of these efforts, however, were initially rejected by state courts and state legislatures, including all efforts to obtain equal marriage rights.

In 1972, in *Baker v Nelson*, the Supreme Court refused to hear an appeal from a Minnesota Supreme Court decision upholding a Minnesota law defining marriage as between a man and a woman, on the grounds that it did not present a federal question.

In other words, marriage was a state's rights issue and the federal Constitution had nothing to say about the matter.

Baker came just five years after the court's landmark decision in *Loving v Virginia*, which struck down Virginia's law banning interracial marriages.

Since the early 20th century, the court has held that certain civil liberties—such as speech, privacy, and the decision about whom to marry—are so fundamental to human dignity and autonomy that they cannot be infringed by state or federal laws.

These fundamental rights are protected by the Fifth and Fourteenth Amendments' prohibition against the deprivation of life, liberty or property without due process of law.

The recognition that the liberty element of the due process clause contains protections for substantive legal rights beyond just the right to physical liberty has been one of the most controversial aspects of 20th-century constitutional jurisprudence.

Marriage cases highlight tension in the theory of "fundamental rights"

These two marriage cases—Baker and Loving—illustrate the due process controversy and created a profound tension in the court's theory of fundamental rights.

Marriage was deemed a fundamental right protected by the US Constitution in Loving, but the prohibition against same-sex marriage was deemed a purely states' rights issue in Baker, making marriage in this case a nonfundamental right.

Ultimately, there is a further question to be asked. Surely a state may impose limitations on certain marriages without running afoul of the Constitution, such as when it prohibits marriages between minors or coerced marriages?

The underlying question in all of these marriage cases, in other words, is figuring out when a state's regulation of marriage is a permissible regulation that furthers important public policies, and when it is an infringement of the fundamental right to marry.

In Obergefell, the majority opinion resolved this tension in favor of Loving, and expressly reversed Baker. But not without controversy.

As the dissenters argued, Loving merely held that traditional marriage (ie, between a man and a woman) cannot be denied on the basis of race. It did not hold that any arrangement that someone wanted to call a "marriage" carries constitutional protections.

But Chief Justice Roberts opined that the majority's decision about the dignity of marriage applied with equal force to plural marriages. He said:

It is striking how much of the majority's reasoning would apply with equal force to the claim of a fundamental right to plural marriage.

Although the decision in Obergefell merely adds same-sex marriages between two consenting adults to the category of marriages protected as a fundamental right, because they are so closely akin to opposite-sex marriages, the chief justice is not off base to recognize that raising marriage to a fundamental right raises the specter of constitutional protections for polygamy.

The court cracks open the equal protection door

At the same time the Supreme Court was developing its robust theory of personal liberties, it was also mapping out a robust theory of the equal protection clause of the Fourteenth Amendment that carefully scrutinized state or federal laws that "classified" people by race, gender, age, alien status, illegitimacy and other immutable characteristics.

Since the 1990s, there has been a strong push by gay-rights advocates to have sexual minorities recognized as a so-called "suspect class" deserving of heightened protections because they have been historically subject to legal and social discrimination.

Just as laws infringing upon fundamental rights are carefully scrutinized by the court, laws that disadvantage certain groups have also been carefully scrutinized by the court under the Fourteenth Amendment's prohibition against denying people the equal protection of the laws.

Laws mandating racial segregation or denying women equal educational opportunities have been struck down on the grounds that race and gender classifications in law do not serve a compelling public purpose.

If sexual minorities were recognized as a suspect class, like racial minorities, then laws treating them differently from the majority population would likely be struck down as unconstitutional.

In all prior gay-rights decisions, however, the Supreme Court has refused to take up the possibility of recognizing sexual minorities as a suspect classification.

This is why the biggest surprise in Obergefell was Justice Kennedy's discussion—albeit brief—of the equal protection implications of same-sex marriage bans.

Justice Kennedy explored the possibility that sexual minorities have equal protection rights when he stated:

> It is now clear that the challenged laws burden the liberty of same-sex couples, and it must be further acknowledged that they abridge central precepts of equality. Here the marriage laws enforced by the respondents are in essence unequal: same-sex couples are denied all the benefits afforded to opposite-sex couples and are barred from exercising a fundamental right. Especially against a long history of disapproval of their relationships, this denial to same-sex couples of the right to marry works a grave and continuing harm. The imposition of this disability on gays and lesbians serves to disrespect and subordinate them. And the Equal Protection Clause, like the Due Process Clause, prohibits this unjustified infringement of the fundamental right to marry.

I predict that it is this passage from Obergefell that will have the most significant legal effect. Its implication is that laws cannot disadvantage gay and lesbian people in their exercise of fundamental liberties, which include not just marriage, but also their rights to safety, employment, housing and educational opportunities.

The fact is that to date, most states do not include provisions in their state laws prohibiting discrimination on the basis of sexual orientation.

The dissenters

Not surprisingly, the four conservatives of the court issued dissents that focused their criticism primarily on the judicial activism of the majority and—as they see it—the blows to democracy and states' rights that occur when the court affirms any individual right as deserving of constitutional protections.

Of course, any time a court strikes down legislation, it is engaging in anti-majoritarian law-making. But that is the point of the Bill of Rights—to protect individuals from the "tyranny of the majority."

And the losers in this debate are already gearing up to represent the issue as one of religious liberties caught in the crossfire.

The majority opinion acknowledged the rights of those who disapprove of same-sex marriage to continue to believe that homosexuality is a sin. Nor are religious groups obliged to perform same-sex marriages. Justice Kennedy explains that,

> The First Amendment ensures that religious organizations and persons are given proper protection as they seek to teach the principles that are so fulfilling and so central to their lives and faiths, and to their own deep aspirations to continue the family structure they have long revered.

But he also acknowledged that their First Amendment rights do not allow them to impose their views on the rest of the population through the coercive arm of the law.

As the religious battleground heats up, the real question, to my mind, is going to be whether the conservatives on the court are willing to maintain the separation of church and state mandated by the First Amendment, which places marriage firmly in the side of secular law.

Same-Sex Parents Should Have Marital Rights

Tanya Washington

Tanya Washington is a professor of law who focuses her research and scholarship on issues related to educational equity and issues arising at the intersection of domestic relations, race, and children's constitutional rights. Her articles have been published in law journals across the nation, including the Harvard Journal for Race and Ethnic Justice, *the* Indiana Law Review, *the* Iowa Journal of Gender, Race and Justice, *the* Utah Law Review, *the* Whittier Journal of Child and Family Advocacy, *the* Hastings Race and Poverty Law Journal, *and the* George Mason University Civil Rights Law Journal.

When the Supreme Court invalidated same-sex marriage bans in June, the Justices acknowledged they had the kids in mind.

In the majority opinion, Justice Kennedy cited the infringement of the interests of children being raised by same-sex couples as one reason for the Court's ruling.

Who are these kids? An estimated 220,000 children under the age of 18 are being raised in same-sex families in the United States. Half are nonwhite.

Protecting kids' rights

My research, scholarship and advocacy efforts have focused on children, particularly black children, for the past 10 years. In an amicus brief filed in Obergefell—the Supreme Court case that ended same-sex marriage bans—my coauthors and I highlighted the legal and economic deprivations children in these families suffer when their parents can't marry.

"The new battleground for same-sex couples is equal rights for their kids," Tanya Washington, The Conversation, October 7, 2015. https://theconversation.com/the-new -battleground-for-same-sex-couples-is-equal-rights-for-their-kids-48062. Licensed under CC BY ND 4.0 International.

We cited landmark Supreme Court cases that make clear that children should not be punished, stigmatized or discriminated against by government action.

Brown v Board of Education, a landmark civil rights case, was one of the cases we relied on because it represents a high-water mark in the Supreme Court's recognition of children's constitutional rights. The plaintiffs in that case were black children asserting their constitutional rights against discrimination by state governments mandating segregated schools.

The Supreme Court cited our amicus brief to support its conclusion that constitutional protection of same-sex marriage affords children "the permanency and stability important to children's best interests."

Despite this acknowledgment, the Supreme Court's opinion is preoccupied with the rights of adults and the expansion of the right to marry. It leaves children in same-sex families at risk.

Legal challenges

Children born into same-sex families frequently are biologically related to only one parent, and the law recognizes only that one parent. The legal status of the child's relationship with her nonbiological parent varies from state to state.

Had the Obergefell decision been more focused on the rights of children in same-sex families, its ruling could have ensured that children's relationships with their nonbiological parents were legally recognized and protected.

However, the opinion failed to reference children's rights explicitly. As a result, as recent developments in state courts reveal, the rights of children in same-sex families remain vulnerable.

No marital presumption

The law referred to as the marital or paternity presumption automatically recognizes a legal parent-child relationship between children born into a marriage and their mothers' husband—

without considering biology. In most states, this law affords legally enforceable rights to both the father and the child.

A New York court recently ruled that the presumption does not apply to same-sex spouses, reasoning that the "presumption of legitimacy ... is one of a biological relationship, not of legal status."

In Florida, three sets of same-sex spouses filed suit in federal court challenging the refusal of state officials to put both parents' names on their children's birth certificates.

Second-parent adoptions and parenting judgments, which are alternative ways of creating a legal parent-child relationship, could protect children's relationships with their nonbiological parents. However, even in the dozen or so states that permit adoptions by same-sex spouses, those adoptions are not always recognized in sister states.

Three months after the Obergefell decision, the Alabama Supreme Court refused to recognize a lesbian mother's adoption of her three nonbiological children granted by a Georgia court in 2007. The court reasoned that Alabama does not need to respect the adoptions because it determined the Georgia court didn't properly apply Georgia law when granting them.

Loss of wealth

Even after the Obergefell decision, children are being deprived of important legal, economic and social benefits and protections that would result from a legal parental relationship with both of their parents.

Children in same-sex families are losing out on worker's compensation benefits, social security benefits, state health insurance, civil service benefits, inheritance and wrongful death proceeds. Denial of these benefits could deprive children of thousands—or in rare cases, even millions—of dollars.

Children can also be deprived of the benefit of parental decision-making authority when it comes to health decisions, securing a passport and registering for school.

Imagine a boy is being raised by two mothers. If his biological mother dies, his "other mother" would have no custody claim. The boy could end up in foster care.

Such laws can have a powerful and adverse financial and legal impact.

According to the Williams Institute, which the Supreme Court cited in Obergefell, same-sex families raising children are twice as likely to earn incomes near the poverty level.

Many of these children are already challenged by experiences informed by their race, ethnicity and socieoeconomic status. Depriving this demographic of important financial and legal protections renders them even more vulnerable. It also compromises the permanency and stability the majority of the Supreme Court recognized as important to children's interests.

The next round of litigation relating to same-sex families should focus on children's rights to legal parentage by both of their parents. Children should be the plaintiffs in these cases, and like the children in Brown v. Board of Education, their rights should command constitutional protection.

The State Should Not Be Involved in Marriages of Any Kind

Stephan Kinsella

Stephan Kinsella is a practicing patent attorney, a libertarian writer and speaker, director of the Center for the Study of Innovative Freedom (C4SIF), and founding and executive editor of Libertarian Papers.

Like everyone, my political and ethical views have evolved over time. From a somewhat racialist milieu in rural Louisiana, I consciously rejected racism when I was in my young teens. From a devout Catholic youth I became a secularist and freethinker at a fairly young age. From libertarian-conservative hawkish Reaganism at 18 I quickly became a die-hard libertarian minarchist, then an anarchist. My initial conservative and Randian pro-American exuberance has given way to a much more critical view of America's baleful effect on world history and my rosy view of its founding has been replaced with skepticism, disdain, scorn, and regret. On abortion, initially militantly pro-choice in the Randian fashion, over the years my aversion to it has grown deeper and deeper to where I see at least late-stage abortion to be tantamount to murder (though I still don't favor its being outlawed by states). On affirmative action, my conservative and libertarian overboard "meritism" has given way to a more contrarian view. My initial attraction to natural rights and natural law type arguments slowly shifted to a more realistic and focused transcendental type approach. On intellectual property, despite my initial—but hesitant and troubled—assumption that it was legitimate, after struggling to find a better way to defend it than arguments such as Rand's and those of utilitarians, I finally rejected it after realizing it is indeed incompatible with property rights. And though I initially praised centralist libertarian ideas such as the Lochner-type caselaw praised by some libertarians I later came to develop a radical skepticism of the wisdom and legitimacy of trusting a central state to monitor state actions. For one more example, despite initially accepting the Hayekian knowledge arguments, I became more skeptical of their coherence in the wake of the Austrian "dehomogenization" debate.

And so it is with gay marriage. My views evolved from mild ambivalence and recommendation of civil unions to an increasingly pro-gay marriage position. And it's become even clearer to me now; I'm no longer reluctant.

Why am I for gay marriage? First, I've never been even slightly homophobic, despite the assumptions of prejudiced "enlightened" liberals (after all, I am from the South!). So that didn't play into the gay marriage issue for me. I was initially somewhat opposed to gay marriage, but not for the standard reasons about it "damaging" the "institution of marriage" and all that malarkey, but because I feared (a) it would instantly grant more positive rights to gay couples, and (b) it was the thin end of the wedge and would be used to argue next for anti-discrimination law being applied to gays, which I of course did and do oppose. I still agree with these concerns, but they are not dispositive.

The basic case for gay marriage is this: in a private order the state would not be involved. Contracts would be enforced by the private legal system, including contracts incidental to consensual regimes such as marriage. Marriage would be a private status recognized socially, with contractual and related legal effects: co-ownership defaults, joint liability presumptions, guardianship assumptions, medical decision and visitation rights, alimony or related default considerations upon termination, and the like. Initially religions and societal custom would regard only heterosexual unions as marriage, but eventually, with secularization of society, gay couples would start being more open, and referring to their partners as spouses, and have "wedding ceremonies." At first mainstream society would be reluctant to accept homosexual unions in the concept or term "marriage," but I suspect that politeness, manners, increasing exposure to and familiarity with open homosexuals (co-workers, family members), and increasing cosmopolitanness and secularization of society would result in an initially grudging including, finally more complete inclusion, perhaps always with a bit of an asterisk among some quarters. Or maybe not, but I think so. In any case the contractual regimes associated with any type of consensual union would be recognized and enforced legally, whether between hetero couples, homosexual couples, spinster sisters, frat buddies, group unions, whatever. The hetero couples, and perhaps one-man-many-wife groupings, would be referred to as marriages, the members as husband and wife. Perhaps the partners in a homosexual union would be referred to as married and spouses; perhaps not. I think so, eventually, but it's irrelevant. There would be no legal battle; capitalist acts among consenting adults would be given legal effect, no matter what the accessory union is named.

But. The state is involved. Even now I think the state should not be involved in marriage, even if it insists on monopolizing the legal system. Ideally, the state should get out of the marriage business and enforce whatever contractual arrangements are ancillary to voluntary unions, whatever the members, whatever society, calls these various unions.

But for now, the state monopolizes the laws and regulations governing co-ownership, child-guardianship and custody issues, medical and death-related decisions and visitation, and the like. And it insists on pigeon-holing the relationships that it will give full contractual effect to in the "marriage" category (which means only that the state uses the word "marriage" in the caption of the statutes giving effect to the consensual arrangements of individuals). So be it. If the state is going to monopolize the legal and court system, if it is going to insist on labeling as "marriage" any relationship whose contractual incidents it will deign to recognize legally, then of course it has no right to deny this to gay couples who wish to have the civil aspects of their relationship legally recognized.

Yes, it's true, this will probably end up with gays getting included in anti-discrimination laws. So what. Abolish the anti-discrimination laws, then.

As for Christian fundamentalists who are so worked up about this: who cares what word the state uses in the caption of the statute giving legal effect to private parties' contracts? If you are opposed to this, stop supporting the state and positive law. (And if you hate evolution being taught in public schools—stop sending your kids there; stop supporting taxation, democracy, the state, and public schools.)

As for the complaint that gay marriage will "harm marriage"— first, nonsense. How is any person's marriage harmed by the choice of word used in the caption of artificial law made by a criminal state? Second, even if it does harm the "institution" of marriage, this is the result of the state monopolizing this area, or of its failure to fully enforce the contractual regimes of non-standard voluntary relationships since they don't fit the traditional definition of marriage—that's no excuse!

As for "purist" libertarians who say we should not extend the reach of the state in this way: well, the state should not have roads either. But would we not oppose a law banning gays from the roads? We would not hide behind, "Well, it's not nice that the state prohibits gays from using the roads, but the solution is not to let gays use the roads—it's to abolish the public roads!" No.

Does gay marriage violate anyone's rights? No. It is not an act of aggression. Does it violate gays' rights to be prevented because of the state's monopolization of the legal system from having their relationships given legal effect? Yes. [N.B.: This whole mess, and other considerations should also highlight for homosexuals why they should also oppose the state and its involvement in this whole area.]

In sum: the state should get out of marriage. If it remains in existence and monopolizes the legal system, it should enforce any contractual aspects of regimes entered into by consenting adults. What they call it is irrelevant. Ideally it would be unlabeled and private society would figure out naming conventions. But the state should not be allowed to hamper the rights of non-standard couples just because it insists on decreeing what is and what is not "marriage." If the state insists on regulating unions and giving it the label "marriage," then gays ought to be able to legally protect their relationships and associated regimes. The state infringes their rights to do this if it monopolizes the field then denies them entrance.

Not only should libertarians support gay marriage, but of course they should.

Same-Sex Marriage Threatens the Entire Human Rights Framework

Travis Weber and L. Lin

Travis Weber is the director of the Center for Religious Liberty at the Family Research Council. He is a graduate of the US Naval Academy, Regent University School of Law, and Georgetown University Law Center, where he studied international law and human rights. L. Lin is a graduate of Harvard Law School who has defended freedom of thought, conscience, and religion for people who hold a variety of beliefs.

April 6, 2016 (ThePublicDiscourse) — In the realm of international human rights law, major conflicts are developing today between freedom of conscience and lesbian, gay, bisexual, and transgender (LGBT) policies. In these conflicts, much more is at stake than the rights of religious people. Everyone who cares about human rights for all—LGBT or not—should be concerned about the resolution of these conflicts, for the continued viability of the entire human rights framework hinges on their outcome.

Conscience occupies a place of paramount importance in international human rights law for at least two reasons. First, our endowment with conscience and reason is the foundation of the human rights system. Second, conscience has also been the engine of human rights activism—from the abolition of slavery to the condemnation of genocide. Because the architects of the modern international human rights system had a high view of conscience, both as evidence of human dignity and as a faculty for discerning moral truth, they identified it as a "core human right."

"Freedom of Conscience and New 'LGBT Rights' in International Human Rights Law", Travis Weber and L. Lin, March 31, 2016. http://www.thepublicdiscourse. com/2016/03/16543/. This piece originally appeared in Public Disclosure, the online journal of the Witherspoon Institute.

Therefore, they created the strongest level of legal protection for it.

As conflicts between freedom of conscience and other interests arose in the past, legal interpreters consistently gave deference to freedom of conscience. Over the past decade, however, conflicts between freedom of conscience and LGBT policies (particularly same-sex marriage and sexual-orientation nondiscrimination mandates) have grown rapidly and now threaten to undermine the status of freedom of conscience.

Conscience in Modern Human Rights Law

The post-World War II generation vowed "never again" after the Holocaust and created a system of international law to protect the human rights of every person. In 1947, the United Nations commissioned individuals from different nations, cultures, and religions to draft the Universal Declaration of Human Rights (UDHR). They could not agree on divinity, but all saw the need for a transcendent basis for human rights, which they outlined in the first Article:

> All human beings are born free and equal in dignity and rights. They are endowed with reason and conscience . . .

The UDHR itself didn't create rights; it merely recognized that they arise from human dignity, reason, and conscience.

The protection of freedom of conscience is strongly expressed in UDHR Article 18:

> Everyone has the right to freedom of thought, conscience and religion; this right includes freedom to change his religion or belief, and freedom, either alone or in community with others and in public or private, to manifest his religion or belief in teaching, practice, worship and observance.

The UN General Assembly further strengthened protection of these freedoms in 1966, when it adopted the legally binding International Covenant on Civil and Political Rights (ICCPR). In that treaty, the right to conscience is one of only seven rights that are "non-derogable"—meaning governments must always respect them, even during public emergencies.

Throughout its history of interpreting the ICCPR, the UN Human Rights Committee (the "Committee"), has described freedom of conscience as "far-reaching and profound." In conflicts between freedom of conscience and interests of the State, the Committee has sought to give the maximum amount of space to individuals to follow their consciences. Why, then, do we have cause for concern?

LGBT Policies in International Law

Recently LGBT policies have proliferated at an incredibly rapid pace. LGBT activists now seek to advance new policies at the United Nations on the basis of sexual orientation and gender identity. Basing new "human rights" on these grounds will open the door to an infinite variety of demands and problems. Where conflicts have arisen, LGBT activists have sought to subordinate freedom of conscience to LGBT policies—a trend that endangers the universal human rights system itself.

All human beings possess rights because of our unique human nature as evidenced by reason and conscience. LGBT persons have the same human rights as others, because of their human dignity, evidenced by their endowed reason and conscience—not by virtue of their sexual attraction or gender preferences.

Some may claim, as then-Secretary of State Hillary Clinton did, that *"gay rights are human rights and human rights are gay rights."* This statement misleads by (1) implying that same-sex-attracted and transgendered persons do not currently enjoy human rights protections, and (2) suggesting that all LGBT claims merit recognition as new human rights. Secretary Clinton has pointed to tragic attacks on same-sex attracted and transgendered persons. Yet no one can credibly assert that LGBT persons do not have human rights. The UDHR and ICCPR protect every individual from arbitrary arrest, torture, and extrajudicial killing by the State, because all humans have *human dignity*, regardless of their sexual attraction or gender preference. If any person is denied these rights (whether they identify as same-sex attracted or not), then UN human rights bodies should investigate and strengthen enforcement of their rights. Secretary Clinton names a problem that already has a solution.

The LGBT movement's attempts to focus exclusively on violence against persons who identify as part of that community, however, injects bias into and undermines the impartial nature of the human rights system. Violence against heterosexuals is equally unjust.

Such claims also misleadingly imply that the claims of LGBT activists are co-extensive with existing human rights. This is not true, however, as LGBT activists claim many new human rights on the grounds of sexual attraction and gender preference.

The LGBT roadmap for effecting change in international human rights law is the Yogyakarta Principles (YP). Described by Human Rights Watch as "groundbreaking," LGBT activists are using the YP to press for "sexual orientation" to be read into all human rights treaties and documents. The YP cites "sexual orientation and gender identity" as "integral to every person's dignity and humanity." Based on this new understanding of human dignity, the YP says "States may incur *additional obligations* as human rights law continues to evolve."

LGBT activists do not base human dignity on reason and conscience, but rather on their sexuality. Yet once rights and "additional obligations" can be created based on sexual and gender preferences, they can become endless—and ultimately meaningless.

LGBT Policies and the Right to Marriage

Of the many policies that LGBT activists assert, the one that has come into sharpest conflict with freedom of conscience is the asserted right to same-sex marriage. UDHR Article 16 states:

> Men and women of full age, without any limitation due to race, nationality or religion, have the right to marry and to found a family. They are entitled to equal rights as to marriage, during marriage and at its dissolution. . . . The family is the natural and

fundamental group unit of society and is entitled to protection by society and the State.

In 1948, the drafters of the UDHR were certainly describing the concept of marriage as between one woman and one man. The drafters took care to note that the institution of marriage and "family" (referring to a mother and a father) was a "natural and fundamental" group unit that both State and society should protect. Yet now, around the world and at the United Nations, LGBT activists seek to redefine Article 16 to include marriages between two men and two women.

In 2013, the European Court of Human Rights (ECHR) upheld decisions by the British government to force a civil servant to provide marriage certificates and a counselor to provide psycho-sexual counseling to same-sex couples. Both had co-workers who were willing to provide these services. Yet the ECHR found that their employers rightfully terminated them because they were obligated to uphold "equality." In doing so, the ECHR rejected the deference historically provided to conscience in the UN framework, and elevated the assertion of "equality" above freedom.

No true, universal human right grounded in human dignity would ever lead to the violation of other human rights. However, the LGBT movement's efforts to limit debate of its claimed "rights" do just that—by limiting freedom of conscience. YP Principle 21(b) states that governments must "[e]nsure that the expression, practice and promotion of *different opinions, convictions and beliefs* with regard to issues of sexual orientation or gender identity" not be "undertaken in a manner incompatible with human rights." The vague phrase "incompatible with human rights" justifies censoring those who hold "different opinions, convictions and beliefs" and violating their freedom of conscience.

How LGBT Policies Could Alter the Balance between the State and the Individual

In 2011, a State Department official responded to a UN declaration on LGBT policies with the following:

> That is the way these international norms are built . . . It's not from scratch. It builds up over time. So this is really a critical beginning of a universal recognition of a new set of rights that forms part of the international system.

This statement is based on the view that the State or the United Nations is the source of our human rights. Charles Malik, one of the drafters of the UDHR, warned after World War II that when the State has the ultimate power to create rights, it also has the power to revoke them. Only when human rights are grounded in transcendent, fixed authority can they stand the test of time and shifts in power. If LGBT policies are elevated above freedom of conscience, it will be to the detriment of all human rights. Our consciences are the basis of our dignity upon which we can claim to have universal and inalienable rights that are not derived from the State.

We should not be too quick to alter the existing structure that so many built so carefully over such a long span of time. Moral convictions in the human conscience led to the recognition of the inalienable and inherent nature of human rights for all. Demoting freedom of conscience to elevate LGBT policies will cause irreversible damage to the entire human rights system. If freedom of conscience is subjugated to LGBT policies, how will the human rights system be sustained?

Traditional Marriage Promotes the Common Good

Unam Sanctam Catholicam

Unam Sanctam Catholicam is a website dedicated to fostering respect and understanding of the sacred traditions of the Catholic Church.

The debate over same-sex marriage has not been settled in this country. Instead, the militant homosexual lobby has simply declared that the debate is over and is trying to shut down conversation. The manner in which they are bullying their opposition into silence is by pushing the idea of homosexual marriage as a "civil right." This is manifestly false, but has unfortunately been repeated so much that ignorant Americans are starting to accept it as a given. Of course, if one admits that homosexual marriage is a "civil right," then to deny the legitimacy of same-sex marriage puts one in the same category as racists who would deny blacks the right to vote—and as we will see, advocates of same-sex marriage are pushing comparisons to the old Jim Crow laws against race mixing to frighten their opponents into silence. In this article, we will examine why homosexual marriage is in no way a "civil right." We will also confine ourselves to using arguments from law and common sense, because in the public debate on this issue, religious and moral considerations are often not given any weight, which is unfortunate.

In the first place we must revisit the concept of a right and from whence any given rights proceed. We hear of various sorts of rights all the time; "human rights," "civil rights," "First Amendment rights," "riparian rights," "right of possession," and so on. A "human right" is a right that we possess by virtue of simply being human, like the right to life. A "First Amendment right" is a right whose

"Homosexual Marriage Is Not a Civil Right," Unam Sanctam Catholicam. Reprinted by permission.

origin is found in the First Amendment to the United States Constitution. "Riparian rights" are those rights to the usage of water that one possesses by virtue of living on the shore of a river or lake (Latin: *riparia*, "shore"). A "right of possession" is the right to use and benefit that is derived from the fact of legal possession of some good.

Keeping this all in mind, a "civil right" is a right that is possessed by virtue of belonging to the *cives*, the "commonwealth," or to put it more simply, a right that one possesses by virtue of their citizenship in a state (Latin: *civitas*, "citizenship"). In the United States, these would be those rights enshrined in the Bill of Rights, of course, but more importantly for this discussion, those derived from the 14th Amendment's promise of "equal protection under the law" and "due process" for all citizens. So a civil right, then, is a right one possesses by virtue of possessing citizenship in this country, as formalized in the 14th Amendment's promise of equal protection.

The question then becomes: Is homosexual marriage something that one has a right to simply by virtue of citizenship?

Here is where the crux of the argument lies, because a civil right only guarantees the *fact* of a particular right, not the *content* implied in the exercise of that right. For example, civil law upholds the rights of contracts to be entered into and enforced, but says nothing about the content of such contracts. Law defends the right of private ownership but says nothing about the particular objects a person owns. It defends the right of employers to enter into employment agreements with employees and for people to freely look for work, but says very little about the sorts of work people may engage in or the particular types of agreements they might make.

Now, while the right to make a contract, the right to engage in employment, and the right to secure private ownership, are all civil rights, the details, or the *content* of such issues fall under the realm of various other bodies of law—business law, labor law, property law, and so on. Thus, while a man might justly argue that being denied the right to seek employment is a violation of his civil rights, he could not argue that his employer's failure to, say, provide him with appropriate protective gear for his job is a violation of a civil right. Civil rights guarantee the fact of him being able to seek employment; the details or content of his employment are regulated by labor law. The appropriate legal channel to address questions of the safety of a workplace would not be through appeals to civil rights, but to labor law. Civil rights only guarantee one the fact of being able to enter into employment, not the conditions or details of that employment.

Applied to marriage, then, the right of persons to enter into the married state has always been recognized as a civil right, but the content or details of who one might marry and under what condition have always been considered subject to State marriage law. It would be a denial of a civil right to tell someone, "You cannot enter into the married state," but it is not a denial of civil rights to assert that the State has the right and public interest of regulating *to whom* and *under what conditions* the married state can be entered into. That falls to marriage law, which is a just function of State government.

Thus all persons retain the civil right to enter into the married state; this is a fact. Homosexual persons have always possessed the right to enter into the married state—they simply have to marry a person of the opposite sex.

Now, an advocate of homosexual marriage would strongly object to this reasoning, because they would argue that they are denied the right to marry *whomever they choose*. This argument, in fact, demonstrates that homosexual marriage is not a civil right, because it shows that the issue is not about the right to enter into the married state, but the *contents of what constitutes the married state*; it is not about whether homosexuals can marry, but whether people are free to define the married state however they choose. This is why opponents of same-sex marriage have always argued that this issue is about the *formal definition of marriage*, not the violation of a civil right.

But to examine this question further—while a civil right is meant to guarantee equality in particular points of law, that is only one half of the picture. There is an old saying that goes back to Plato—equality for equals, inequality for unequals. In other words, when a right is applied equally to everyone in a given class, it is because it presupposes there are no essential distinctions within that class that would preclude the right from being equally applied. To take an example the same-sex crowd always brings up, this is why the old Jim Crow laws against interracial marriage were struck down as civil rights violations. It was recognized that men were men, and women were women; race is not intrinsic to sexuality, therefore there is no compelling distinction between the races that would preclude them from freely entering into the married state. Essentially, the overturning of the old prohibitions on interracial marriage supports traditional marriage because the law recognized that *any man can marry any woman*. Therefore the racist Jim Crow marriage laws were true instances of civil inequality because they were proposing distinctions in the application of rights which were in fact irrelevant; any man is capable of entering into marriage with any woman, and the right for any man to enter into the married state with any woman could not be infringed.

However, this is not to say that there are not cases when a true distinction arises which necessitates a different approach. For example, every doctor has a right to be able to seek employment, but not any person has the right to claim to be a doctor. A person without a medical license is not entitled to the same privileges and rights to practice medicine as a person with one, and it is no denial of civil rights to say this because whether or not one is a licensed doctor is intrinsic to what it means to practice medicine in our society. A person without a college degree cannot claim the rights of a person with a college degree, nor can a person without a security clearance claim the rights and privileges that come with a security clearance. Persons without these qualifications are treated unequally from persons who have them, because the possession of such credentials are intrinsic to these classes of individuals.

We all understand that these are real distinctions intrinsic to the occupations or situations they are relative to, and that it is no discrimination or civil rights violation to say that these distinctions make a true difference. This is because we are not dealing with an artificially imposed inequality, but simply with the *boundaries of certain definitions*. The definition of a lawyer is one who is licensed to practice law, and to say as much does not imply any prejudice against those whose profession does not include licensing to practice law. To definition of a college graduate is one who has a college degree, and to say so—and to reflect the fact in law—implies no prejudice against those whose credentials do not include a college degree.

We see, then, that this does come back to *definitions*. The same-sex marriage lobby has skirted the question of the definition of marriage by arguing the universal right for any person to marry any other person. It does little good to argue for same-sex marriage as a civil right whilst simultaneously avoiding the question of defining the institution of marriage. Obviously, the same-sex marriage lobby has done this because they can offer no definition of marriage which would allow for gay marriage while excluding other even less savory arrangements (polygamy, polyandry, incest, pedophilia, etc).

It is commonly understood that marriage is a unique relationship that is permanent and presumptively procreative, which means that it involves sexual intercourse. Not all types of relationship involve sexual intercourse; friendships may be very strong, ties of blood, professional relationships—all may be strong, but they are not marital because they do not involve sexual intercourse. And that is fine. *To say the marital relationship must include sexual intercourse involves no prejudice against those whose relationships do not include intercourse.* And, unlike race, the ability to engage in sexual intercourse is *intrinsic* to what marriage is, and because the ability to engage in intercourse is dependent upon gender, gender is absolutely intrinsic and central to marriage. There is no civil rights violation in simply asserting this is the case.

What is really at stake here is whether the definition of marriage will move from the objective to the realm of the subjective. In the pushing of an alleged "civil right" to enter into homosexual marriage, the pro-gay lobby is arguing for an understanding of marriage that is based purely on the consent of two parties regardless of any objective criteria—the right to define reality as they see fit and compel the public to accept these arbitrary definitions and enshrine them in law.

Of course, such an interpretation is profoundly subjective and personal, reflecting the modern error of presuming that marriage is a purely private arrangement with no public purpose. On the other hand, the traditional conjugal definition of marriage acknowledges that government issues marriage licenses because *marriage serves a public purpose.* We know that when men and women come together they have sex, and sex makes babies. This has tremendous consequences for the common welfare, and so government wants to unite men and women and tie them to any children born of their union. Marriage is an exclusive, presumptively procreative and permanent contract between a man and a woman, which regenerates society and provides enormous benefits for the common good.

This means that *marriage is not, from a civil perspective, the public affirmation of love.* If this were the case, government would be issuing love licenses, not marriage licenses, and this is obvious since friendships or courtships are not issued licenses. So marriage's public purpose is to unite a relationship that is potentially life-giving, legally binding parents to the children they create. This sort of union can only exist in the traditional concept of marriage and not to any other union. As we have said above, it is no denial of anybody's civil rights to assert that the right to claim the status of marriage can only exist within this context; the fact that it does not apply to other sorts of relationships is no more a violation of civil rights than it is to say a person without a medical license cannot practice medicine. Custom has never viewed the question in this sense, nor have legal scholars ever interpreted the 14th Amendment to establish a civil right for anyone to enter into marriage with any other person based on mere consent. The Reconstruction Congress who passed the 14th Amendment after the Civil War would probably have an apoplectic fit if they were told that their legislation would one day be used to affirm the legal right of men to marry men.

As to subsidiary questions of visiting rights at hospitals, end of life decisions, etc. these can be addressed through existing legislation relating to durable power of attorney, inheritance law, etc. They are not relevant to questions of marriage law or civil rights.

To sum up: a civil right is a right that a person possesses by virtue of their citizenship in the state. Civil rights pertain to the fact of having a particular right (to marry, work, have recourse to the law, etc) but do not deal with the content of such arrangements. Because any person has the right to enter into the married state, the right to gay marriage is not a civil rights violation. Any person can enter into the married state, but not under any circumstances they may choose. The question is not one of civil rights but of the definition of marriage, which is what homosexual activists contest. Since gender difference and sexual intercourse is intrinsic to understanding the institution of marriage, it is no discrimination of civil rights to say that the married state cannot be conferred on those whose relationships do not involve sexual intercourse. Ultimately the argument devolves to the definition of marriage and whether it is a private, subjective concept or a public, objective concept. The traditional conjugal definition of marriage understands marriage as a public good, the details of which are regulated by law in accord with promoting the common good. The homosexual proposition of marriage relegates it to the realm of a private arrangement dictated by mere consent, a definition which is so broad as to allow for no non-arbitrary reason for not admitting other types of unions as marriage as well.

Do Transgender Individuals Deserve Special Protection?

Overview: US Courts Debate the Difference Between Sex Equality and Gender Equality

Lyle Denniston

Lyle Denniston is the Supreme Court correspondent for the National Constitution Center, a nonprofit organization dedicated to disseminating information about the US Constitution.

The Statements at Issue:

"The Department of Justice has for some time now made clear that sex discrimination includes discrimination against transgender people—that is, discrimination based on gender identity. That is consistent not only with the language of the statutes, but also with the legal interpretations adopted by federal courts—including the appellate court with jurisdiction over the state of North Carolina. There is nothing radical or even particularly unusual about the notion that the word 'sex' includes the concept of 'gender.'"

— *Excerpts from remarks on Monday by Vanita Gupta, head of the Justice Department's Civil Rights Division, as she announced the filing of a federal government lawsuit against state officials and agencies in North Carolina, seeking to block enforcement of the state's "HB 2" law regulating access to toilet and changing rooms for public employees and students. The lawsuit was filed in Winston-Salem.*

"The Justice Department's position is a baseless and blatant overreach. This is an attempt to unilaterally rewrite long-established federal civil rights laws in a manner that is wholly inconsistent with the intent of Congress and disregards decades of statutory interpretation by the courts. The overwhelming weight of legal authority recognizes that transgender status is not a protected class under [federal job rights law]."

"Do existing federal civil rights laws already protect transgender people?" Lyle Denniston, Constitution Daily, May 10, 2016. Reprinted with permission.

— Excerpt from the text of a lawsuit that the governor and the state public safety director of North Carolina filed on Monday against the federal government and Justice Department officials, seeking a federal court ruling to make it definite and clear that existing federal civil rights protection does not apply to transgender people. The lawsuit was filed in Elizabeth City, N.C.

The Current State of the Law on this Point Is ...

The mandate that government should treat the sexes equally, especially in access to public benefits, can be traced to constitutional law and theory, and also to federal civil rights laws. But neither development has run its course yet, so it is an exaggeration to say that there is unanimity, in the courts or elsewhere, on when one's sex, or gender, can be used to discriminate.

The constitutional origins of sex-based equality certainly go back at least to the 19th Amendment, in 1920, extending voting rights to women. However, equality did not become a broader civil rights requirement until a pioneering—though factually narrow—Supreme Court decision in 1971, giving women the equal right to handle a relative's estate.

That decision, in the case of *Reed v. Reed*, was the first to apply the Constitution's guarantee of the "equal protection of the laws" to achieve equality of the sexes as a general proposition.

In reality, because the proposed Equal Rights Amendment never was ratified, there is still not a full constitutional promise of equality of the sexes, because discrimination based on sex does not have to satisfy the toughest constitutional test, the way that race bias must.

Equality of the sexes has grown more rapidly, and more widely, through passage of laws by Congress. It is out of those laws that has sprung—but only in very recent years—the idea that sex equality actually can also mean "gender equality." And that development has produced the current controversy over protecting "gender identity," for transgender people. It is much too early, though, to say that its dimensions in federal civil rights law are clear or well established.

To digress for a moment: what is the difference between sex equality (the kind specifically promised in federal civil rights laws) and gender equality (not specifically mentioned in those laws)? The former basically depends upon biological characteristics, distinctly separating male from female. The latter depends upon an individual's own internal sense, not gender at birth, of being male or female. Is the word "sex" in the federal anti-bias laws confined only to the former?

At this point, if transgender rights are to exist or to expand, they almost certainly will do so primarily through interpretations of federal civil rights laws, not through interpretations of equality guarantees in the Constitution. No court has yet ruled that transgender equality is in any way promised by the nation's basic charter. And, with proponents of transgender rights having available at least an argument that the existing laws banning discrimination based on sex do, or should, protect transgender people, courts will largely steer themselves away from constitutional judgments.

There are three federal civil rights laws now figuring in the transgender rights movement. The federal government brought all three of those to bear on Monday when it sued state officials and agencies in North Carolina, to stop enforcement of a law that strictly limits the toilet and changing room facilities that transgender people may use in that state. The law, "HB 2," mainly requires a transgender person to use a gender-designated facility for one born male or female, not based on an individual's actual gender identity.

The three laws are Title VII of the 1964 Civil Rights Act, which bans workplace bias based upon sex, and two laws that ban sex bias in programs funded with federal tax dollars: Title IX of a federal educational benefits law passed in 1972, and a 2013 provision of the Violence Against Women Act. Individually, and taken together, those laws—according to Justice Department officials—definitely ban discrimination based on a transgender person's "gender identity." (The law that has been applied most expansively in that way is Title VII, primarily because of the energetic use of that law for the past four years by the federal Equal Employment Opportunity Commission in job bias cases.)

Hours before the federal lawsuit relying upon those laws was filed in one city in North Carolina, the governor and another top state official sued the federal government in another city.

For months, federal Justice Department officials have been arguing that there is a strong trend now running in federal court decisions in favor of transgender rights under those statutes, and that court rulings against those rights are now quite dated.

The state officials' lawsuit argued that the federal government is seeking a "radical" expansion of civil rights law, without any change in the law by Congress. That lawsuit is aimed at getting a clear-cut ruling that only Congress has the authority to confer legal rights on transgender people, at the federal level.

Those lawsuits will go forward independently, at least for the time being, as will another challenge to "HB 2" that was filed in federal court in March. It may take some time, but the deep controversy over transgender equality no doubt will work its way up to the Supreme Court, from North Carolina or elsewhere. This is one of the hottest topics of the day on civil rights.

Transgender People Face High Rates of Workplace Discrimination

Crosby Burns and Jeff Krehely

Crosby Burns is a special assistant and Jeff Krehely is director of the LGBT Research and Communications Project at the Center for American Progress.

Gay and transgender individuals continue to face widespread discrimination in the workplace.* Studies show that anywhere from 15 percent to 43 percent of gay people have experienced some form of discrimination and harassment at the workplace. Moreover, a staggering 90 percent of transgender workers report some form of harassment or mistreatment on the job. These workplace abuses pose a real and immediate threat to the economic security of gay and transgender workers.

Congress should work quickly to pass the Employment Non-Discrimination Act, or ENDA, to ensure that all Americans are judged in the workplace based on their skills, qualifications, and the quality of their work. Right now, too many of our country's gay and transgender workers are being judged on their sexual orientation and gender identity—factors that have no impact on how well a person performs their job.

The numbers

The Williams Institute on Sexual Orientation Law and Public Policy aggregated a number of surveys to determine the extent to which gay and transgender workers experience discrimination and harassment in the workplace. Their findings illustrate that discrimination and harassment are pervasive:

- Fifteen percent to 43 percent of gay and transgender workers have experienced some form of discrimination on the job.
- Eight percent to 17 percent of gay and transgender workers report being passed over for a job or fired because of their sexual orientation or gender identity.
- Ten percent to 28 percent received a negative performance evaluation or were passed over for a promotion because they were gay or transgender.
- Seven percent to 41 percent of gay and transgender workers were verbally or physically abused or had their workplace vandalized.

Straight coworkers also attest to the presence of discrimination and harassment against LGBT workers. The Williams Institute's report found that 12 percent to 30 percent of straight workers witnessed discrimination in the workforce based on sexual orientation.

Controlled experiments have found consistent evidence of workplace discrimination as well. When researchers send two sets of matched resumes to major employers, and one indicates the applicant is gay, employers warmly receive "gay" resumes far less often than "straight" resumes. Seven out of eight of these studies confirmed the existence of antigay employment discrimination.

Transgender individuals encounter workplace discrimination and harassment at even higher rates than gays and lesbians. Earlier this year, the National Center for Transgender Equality and the National Gay and Lesbian Task Force released a comprehensive study on transgender discrimination that revealed near universal problems at the workplace:

- Ninety percent of transgender individuals have encountered some form of harassment or mistreatment on the job.
- Forty-seven percent of workers have experienced an adverse job outcome because they are transgender. This includes:

    o Forty-four percent who were passed over for a job

    o Twenty-three percent who were denied a promotion

    o And 26 percent who were fired because they were transgender

The stories behind the numbers

Behind these statistics are the heartbreaking stories of everyday Americans losing their jobs based on characteristics that have nothing to do with their job performance.

Vandy Beth Glenn lost her job with the Georgia General Assembly when her boss fired her because she was transgender:

> [My boss] told me I would make other people uncomfortable, just by being myself. He told me that my transition was unacceptable. And over and over, he told me it was inappropriate. Then he fired me. I was escorted back to my desk, told to clean it out, then marched out of the building…I was devastated.

Brook Waits was gainfully employed in Dallas, Texas until her manager fired her immediately after she saw a picture on Brook's cell phone of Brook and her girlfriend kissing on New Year's Eve:

> I didn't lose my job because I was lazy, incompetent, or unprofessional. Quite the contrary, I worked hard and did my job very well. However that was all discarded when my boss discovered I am a lesbian. In a single afternoon, I went from being a highly praised employee, to out of a job.

And officer Michael Carney was denied reinstatement as a police officer in Springfield, Massachusetts because he told his supervisors that he was gay:

> I'm a good cop. But I've lost two and a half years of employment fighting to get that job back because I'm gay…I'm proud to be Irish-American. I'm proud to be gay, and I'm proud to be a cop in Springfield, MA.

The economic consequences of discrimination

Gay and transgender individuals suffer from socioeconomic inequalities in large part due to pervasive discrimination in the workplace. Discrimination directly causes job instability and high turnover, resulting in greater unemployment and poverty rates for gay and transgender people, as well as the wage gap between gay and straight workers.

Consider that gay men earn 10 percent to 32 percent less than similarly qualified heterosexual males. Older gay and lesbian adults experience higher poverty rates than their heterosexual counterparts. And transgender individuals are twice as likely to be unemployed and are four times as likely to live in poverty. Nearly 20 percent have been or are currently homeless.

Companies should care about these numbers if they are in the business of boosting profits. Time and again, researchers have demonstrated that discrimination diminishes productivity, job satisfaction, and the mental and physical health of all employees.

Enacting legislation that provides real protection

Gay and transgender individuals' legal and social standing is improving despite their unfair and unequal treatment in the workplace. An increasing number of states, municipalities, and businesses have adopted nondiscrimination protections that prohibit discrimination based on sexual orientation and gender identity.

The public, too, has increasingly voiced support for employment protections and workplace fairness for gay and transgender workers. And more and more gay workers are coming out at the workplace, a sign that workplace climates have become more accepting or at least tolerant overall.

Nevertheless, gay and transgender people continue to lack full workplace protections afforded to women, people of color, veterans, seniors, and the disabled. Under federal law it is still legal to fire someone for being gay or transgender. Where state or local laws exist, gay and transgender workers file discrimination complaints at comparable rates and in some case higher rates than other protected classes such as gender and race. But Congress has thus far failed to incorporate gay and transgender workers into employment laws that shield these and other groups from workplace discrimination nationwide.

Lawmakers in both chambers of the 112th Congress recently introduced ENDA, which would finally bring full workplace protections to nearly all of our nation's workforce. If passed, gay and transgender workers would have similar protections that were afforded to other minority groups with the passage of the Civil Rights Act of 1964 and the Americans with Disabilities Act. And while comprehensive in scope, ENDA explicitly exempts religious organizations and small businesses with less than 15 employees, prohibits preferential treatment for gay and transgender workers, and does not require employers to offer domestic partner benefits to employees' same-sex partners.

ENDA's premise is simple: All Americans deserve equal treatment in the workplace regardless of sexual orientation or gender identity. Lawmakers should swiftly enact ENDA to level the playing field for all American workers, gay or straight, transgender or not.

Gay and transgender individuals comprise a significant part of the American labor force. Every day, they go to work to make an honest living to support themselves and their families, and help our economy grow along the way. But far too many go to work with the fear that they will lose their job based on factors that have nothing to do with their job performance and ability.

Discrimination has no place in our society or in our workplaces. Our nation can and should do better for all our workers.

---

*In this column, the term gay is used as an umbrella term for people who identify as lesbian, gay, or bisexual.

Restrooms Are Dangerous Places for Transgender Students

Alison Gash

Alison Gash is an assistant professor of political science at the University of Oregon.

Bathroom safety has become the next battle for transgender students on college campuses across the nation.

Often referred to as "bathroom desegregation," calls for safer bathrooms have inspired "shit-ins" at California Polytechnic and San Diego State, where transgender advocates asked student allies to use only gender-neutral restrooms.

Recently, "urine" blockades also confronted Berkeley students at Sather Gate, the main entrance to campus. Advocates filled plastic cups with fake urine and lined them up to greet students as they crossed the threshold into campus to protest inadequate restrooms for transgender students.

Why all the contention over bathrooms? Recent studies suggest that over 50% of transgender individuals will experience sexual assault in their lifetime (a rate that is far higher than for nontransgendered individuals), and using bathrooms could pose a significant threat of physical harm or harassment.

Fear of violence

Studies show that transgender students could be harassed, sexually assaulted or subjected to other physical violence when they are required to use a gendered bathroom.

One survey, commissioned by the Williams Institute, a think tank at UCLA, found that 68% of participants were subjected to

"Explainer: Why Transgender Students Need 'Safe' Bathrooms," Alison Gash, The Conversation, November 19, 2015. https://theconversation.com/explainer-why -transgender-students-need-safe-bathrooms-50831. Licensed under CC BY ND 4.0 International.

homophobic slurs while trying to use the bathroom. Nine percent confronted physical violence.

Another study that surveyed transgender individuals in Washington, DC found that 70% were either verbally threatened, physically assaulted or prevented in some way from using the bathroom of their choice. Some experienced more than one form of such behavior.

Yet another survey found that 26% of transgender students in New York were denied access to their preferred bathrooms altogether.

Redesigning bathrooms

As a result, transgender students need to constantly weigh the trade-offs as they consider bathroom options.

As one University of Washington student articulates:

> Do I choose physical safety or emotional safety? Do I choose physical health or mental health?

So, from California to Texas, in elementary schools and colleges, administrators are considering the costs and benefits of redesigning bathrooms to accommodate transgender students.

For example, students at University of Pittsburgh can now use bathrooms that conform to their own gender identity. Arizona State University, Ohio State and Wesleyan University, among several others, have instituted policies requiring all new construction to include gender-neutral bathrooms. They are assessing how to modify the existing bathrooms to become gender-neutral single-stall facilities.

This is not limited to colleges and universities. As increasing numbers of primary- and secondary-school-aged children are identifying as transgender, public schools have become "ground zero" for fights over bathroom safety.

Miraloma Elementary School, in San Francisco, for instance, removed gendered signs from many of their bathrooms.

In fact, about two years ago, Governor Jerry Brown signed into law the School Success and Opportunity Act, requiring that all students be able to access bathrooms or locker rooms that are consistent with their own gender identity in California's K-12 settings.

The "bathroom bill" opposition

But as with other issues concerning transgender rights, some have reacted to these changes with visceral opposition.

For instance, Wisconsin, along with several other states, is considering legislation that would require school districts to only provide separate-gendered bathrooms as a way to stop local school districts from accommodating requests from transgender students.

An elementary school student in Stafford County, Virginia, was prohibited from using the bathroom associated with her gender identity after parents and politicians in the state spoke out against the student's request.

In fact, opposition to these bathroom accommodations figured prominently in the initiative to vote down Houston's recent antidiscrimination ordinance, which would have, like hundreds of others across the nation, prohibited discrimination in housing, gender and public accommodations on the basis of sexual orientation and gender identity, among others.

Opponents dubbed it the "bathroom bill," framing the policy as one that would permit "men in women's bathrooms" and would expose women and girls to sexual predators.

Consequently, the ordinance—subjected to public review under court order—failed with 61% of the voters.

This opposition exists even when transgender advocates have not only focused on their own risks but have also invoked the needs of students with disabilities, those who may need "family bathrooms" and students who have survived sexual abuse and are more comfortable with single-stall facilities.

And now, Privacy for All, a group dedicated to opposing transgender bathroom advocacy, is hoping to launch a similar campaign in California. It is currently collecting signatures to bar any public institution from permitting individuals to use bathrooms or changing rooms that comport with their gender identity.

Federal intervention has sent out mixed signals as well. On the one hand, the Department of Education issued a letter to an Illinois school district stating that denying a transgender student's rights to access a bathroom consistent with their gender identity is a violation of Title IX.

On the other hand, a federal court rejected a transgender student's claim that his equal rights were violated when his university rejected his request to use a locker room that matched his gender identity.

Need for safety

At this point, for most transgender students, bathroom options are limited.

Either they have to travel quite a distance to get to the nearest single-stall gender-neutral bathroom, or change in an "alternative" locker room (often a faculty bathroom or custodial closet).

There could even be days when they go to class in their workout clothes or "hold it in." Hence, demonstrating Berkeley students held out signs that said: "Where was I supposed to go?" or "I couldn't hold it any longer."

Such options have clear drawbacks and health risks. Urinary tract infections, depression and even suicide could be among them.

As a result, sometimes students see their best option as renting a house near campus so they can go home to use the bathroom.

As we mark World Toilet Day by campaigning on behalf of the billions of individuals who lack access to safe, clean sanitation, remember that among those denied access to safe bathrooms are transgender students.

Transgender Students Are Protected by Title IX

GLBTQ Legal Advocates & Defenders

GLBTQ Legal Advocates & Defenders is a nonprofit organization that works through the legal system to end discrimination of sexual orientation, HIV status, and gender identity and expression.

Protections for Transgender Students Generally

Safe use of bathrooms and locker rooms in schools and colleges is essential for any student—particularly transgender students, who can face unique challenges. Transgender people are individuals who have a persistent and deeply held identification with a gender that is different from that which they were assigned at birth. Like everyone else, transgender students deserve to use bathrooms and locker room facilities with assurances for their safety and dignity.

In addition, Massachusetts law prohibits public schools and colleges from discriminating against transgender students, including on the bases of sex and disability.[1] For example, in *Pat Doe v. Yunits*,[2] a Superior Court found that a transgender student who was forbidden by her school from wearing clothing that comported with her female gender identity could bring a discrimination action against the school district.

Recent interpretations of state and federal law by courts and government agencies in related contexts make clear that transgender students are protected by existing law. For example, sex discrimination laws have been determined to protect transgender people in employment and credit.[3] The same is true for disability protections in both school and employment settings.[4]

As such, transgender students are guaranteed non-discriminatory treatment at public schools and colleges throughout Massachusetts. This guarantee includes ensuring that transgender

"Transgender Students' Use of Bathroom and Locker Rooms," March 2014. Reprinted with permission.

students have safe and dignified access to the bathroom and locker room facilities that are consistent with each student's gender identity and expression.

Transgender Students' Right to Use Gender-Appropriate Bathrooms

Transgender students should be allowed to use the bathroom that would be appropriate for a non-transgender student with the same gender identity and expression as the transgender student, regardless of the transgender student's birth sex. Most transgender students already do so without anyone needing to be informed of or to scrutinize the student's gender or medical history. The touchstone for equality in this context is equal treatment. Non-transgender students appropriately are not asked for proof of their gender or information relating to their medical history; neither should transgender students be asked for such information. An alternative that would require either anatomical checks or proof of medical history would be insulting, invasive, and would violate the student's right to privacy, particularly with regard to personal medical information.

In addition, forcing transgender students who have transitioned to use the bathroom that matches their assigned birth sex would actually cause more distraction and problems. For example, a female-to-male transgender individual (who has transitioned from female to male by taking hormones with or without any surgical intervention) has a gender presentation that is similar to non-transgender men. Requiring a transgender male student to use the women's room would likely make everyone uncomfortable—the transgender male student as well as the non-transgender female students with whom he would have to share the facility. The same would be true for transgender women. Also, such a policy would be not only degrading and potentially unsafe for the transgender student but seriously damaging to the student's mental health.

Transgender Students' Right to Use Gender-Appropriate Locker Rooms

While some locker rooms can pose a slightly different situation, transgender students should be allowed to use the locker room that would be appropriate for a nontransgender student with the same gender identity and expression.

Like most people, transgender people seek privacy and personal space when changing and showering in locker rooms, in order to protect their own safety and privacy. Just as is true for many non-transgender individuals, many transgender individuals have a strong sense of modesty and choose to use private shower stalls when available and enclosed bathroom stalls to change their clothes. As is also true for non-transgender individuals, not everyone is as modest.

In situations where nudity may be unavoidable, and a transgender student has expressed discomfort with this situation, schools and colleges can make a reasonable accommodation by creating a separate changing/showering space within the locker room—as many do already for people with physical disabilities. This solution may be as easy as putting up a shower curtain, or it may involve creating a separate shower stall or changing space that is private. Either way, schools and colleges should work with the transgender student/s to find an accommodation that is both reasonable and appropriate for the student, and that does not require the student to use an inappropriate facility.

An inappropriate facility would be one that is not consistent with the student's gender identity and expression. For example, it would not be appropriate for a school to require a student who has a male gender identity and expression (even if that student was born female) to use the locker room facility provided for female students. Neither would it be appropriate for a school to require a student who has a female gender identity and expression (even if that student was born male) to use the locker room facility provided for male students.

As a last resort, if no reasonable accommodation that satisfies the student's concern can be made within the locker room that is consistent with the student's gender identity and expression, then a school or college can make available a separate, single user locker room and showering facility.

Summary

In general, we have found at GLAD that most people do not encounter problems with transgender people using bathrooms and locker room facilities. To the extent we have learned of problems, we have found that appropriate education and/or training can resolve them. Often, resolving a concern that gets raised either by a transgender or non-transgender person in this context is as easy as educating staff or students about the basic realities and existence of transgender people's lives. Having appropriate policies in place to begin with can help prevent any problems from arising. The Massachusetts Department of Elementary and Secondary Education (DESE) has issued guidance that public schools should put in place for their transgender students that include allowing them to use the bathroom and locker room that corresponds to their gender identity.

Resources

1. *See* Mass. Gen. L. c. 76, sec. 5 (prohibiting discrimination "in obtaining the advantages, privileges and courses of study" on account of sex); Mass. Const. Pt. 1, Art. I, X and CXIV (state constitutional prohibition of unequal treatment based upon sex and disability).
2. 2001 WL 664947 (Mass. Super. Ct. Feb. 26, 2001).
3. *See Millett v. Lutco*, 2001 WL 1602800 (Mass. Comm'n Against Discrimination) (Massachusetts law prohibiting discrimination on the basis of sex encompasses discrimination against transgender individuals); *Rosa v. Parks West Bank & Trust Co.*, 214 F.3d 213 (1st Cir. 2000) (a transgender person denied a bank application for a loan could sue under the Equal Credit Opportunity Act's sex discrimination protections).
4. *See Pat Doe,* 2001 WL 664947 at *5 (finding that state constitutional disability protections covered a transgender student seeking to wear clothing that comported with her female gender identity); *Jette v. Honey Farms*, 2001 WL 1602799 (Mass. Comm'n Against Discrimination) (holding that Massachusetts disability protections in employment covers transgender employees).

Transgender Restroom Laws Protect Citizens

Brandon Morse

Brandon Morse is a blogger on RedState, a conservative political blog.

The media's new favorite pastime is talking about how corporations and celebrities are boycotting states like Mississippi, and North Carolina due to what they're calling "anti-LGBT" bills. If the media was reporting honestly, they'd tell you they're anything but. That's not important, however. What's important is that pop-culture's favorite punching bag, the Christians, are once again painted as villains.

Funny enough, while Mississippi's bill does protect the rights of the religious by allowing them to deny catering to, or hosting services which may go against their religious beliefs—and not at all about keeping the gays down—North Carolina's bathroom bill has absolutely nothing to do with religion.

As I've said before when PayPal withdrew its plans to plant a global HQ from North Carolina, this is not a law that was passed for the sake of hating on transgendered individuals, and everything to do with keeping women and girls safe from creeps, perverts, and worse. Transgender activists say that no transgendered individual has ever assaulted anyone in the history of ever. Media Matters likes to claim that the idea of a transgendered bathroom predator has been debunked, because a group of people said so on the Daily Show...you know...the comedy news program.

Trouble is, while transgendered people in particular might not be sexual offenders, there are plenty of people out there who would take advantage of a law that would allow men into women's restrooms. I know that, because with a quick Google search, I was spoiled for choice on story after story of a man being

"This Is Why We Need Transgender Bathroom Laws," Brandon Morse, RedState, April 11, 2016. Reprinted with permission.

busted for spying on women in the bathroom, some of them even claiming transgenderism.

In fact, here are just four examples that happened recently:

1. Man Dressed as Woman Arrested for Spying Into Mall Bathroom Stall, Police Say—VA, Nov 17th, 2015
2. California Man Dressed as Woman Busted for Videoing in Women's Bathroom—CA, Apr 10th, 2016
3. Man Strips In Women's Restroom, Says New Transgender Rules Make It Totally Legal—WA, Feb 17th 2016
4. Sexual predator jailed after claiming to be "transgender" to assault women in shelter—Toronto, Mar 4th 2014

Again, these are just four that I found with a light Google search. There were more that had men not even pretending to be women to get in, and just straight up doing it. None of these people may have actually been trans, but it doesn't matter? They utilized trying to look like women in order to gain access to the privacy of women and girls.

Imagine what it would look like if doing this was legal, which is exactly what North Carolina was trying to avoid. The media and transgender activists can throw around words like "civil rights," and "bigotry" around all day. But in the grand scheme, they should really stop for a moment and take a look at what would follow them through the door should they open it.

Kaeley Triller, a rape survivor, actually faced the worst of consequences as a girl. She wrote about it in an article at *The Federalist.*

"I read these reports, and my heart starts to race. They can't be serious. Let me be clear: I am *not* saying that transgender people are predators. Not by a long shot. What I *am* saying is that there are countless deviant men in this world who will pretend to be transgender as a means of gaining access to the people they want to exploit, namely women and children. It already happens. Just Google Jason Pomares, Norwood Smith Burnes, or Taylor Buehler, for starters."

She's wholly correct, and that's the point of the transgender bathroom laws. It's not targeting transgendered people, it's targeting the scum that would use the identity to hurt people. Triller continues...

"Even if there aren't hundreds of abusers rushing into locker rooms by the dozens, the question I keep asking myself is, 'What if just one little girl gets hurt by this? Would that be enough to make people reconsider it?'"

And I believe that's a fair question to ask. With proof already available to us that harm *will* occur, why do corporations, celebrities, and activists still push against the laws? They claim they're fighting for equality, but I don't see any equality in men assaulting women while they're most vulnerable. They say they're fighting against bigotry, but I just see them standing against people who want to see to it that what happened to people like Triller, doesn't happen to other little girls.

In the end, we all have to weigh which is more important, the feelings of some transgendered individuals, or the physical safety and emotional well being of women and girls.

Organizations to Contact

The editors have compiled the following list of organizations concerned with the issues debated in this book. The descriptions are derived from materials provided by the organizations. All have publications or information available for interested readers. This list was compiled on the date of publication of the present volume; the information provided here may change. Be aware that many organizations take several weeks or longer to respond to inquiries, so allow as much time as possible.

Advocates for Youth
2000 M Street NW, Suite 750
Washington, DC 20036
(202) 419-3420
website: http://www.advocatesforyouth.org

Advocates for Youth is an organization that helps young people make informed and responsible decisions about their reproductive and sexual health. The agency's website includes information on sexuality, relationship abuse, policy and advocacy, and violence and harassment.

American Civil Liberties Union (ACLU)
125 Broad Street, 18th Floor
New York, NY 10004
(212) 549-2500
website: http://www.aclu.org

The American Civil Liberties Union is a nonpartisan not-for-profit organization that works in the courts, legislatures, and communities to defend and preserve the individual rights and civil liberties guaranteed to all people in the US by the Constitution and laws of the US. The ACLU website includes information on recent legislative actions, Supreme Court cases involving the ACLU, and reports and commentaries by ACLU members.

Campus Pride
PO Box 240473
Charlotte, NC 28224
(704) 277-6710
website: http://www.campuspride.org

Campus Pride is a not-for-profit organization for LGBTQ college students and their allies. It works to develop student leaders, campus networks, and campus actions to create positive change on campus and in communities. The Campus Pride website provides resources for students to create a safe, LGBTQ-friendly college campus community.

Center for Black Equity (CBE)
PO Box 77313
Washington, DC 20013
(202) 641-8527
website: http://centerforblackequity

CBE is an institution committed to supporting leaders, institutions, and programs for health, economic, and social equity for LGBT people of African descent. CBE provides resources for local advocacy projects concerning such issues as HIV/AIDS, hate crimes, violence reduction, voter registration, and community organizing.

Equality Federation
818 SW 3rd Avenue, #141
Portland, OR 97204-2405
(929) 373-3370
website: http://www.equalityfederation.org

Equality Federation is a partner organization for state organizations that advocate for lesbian, gay, bisexual, transgender, and queer people. Equality Federation assists local leaders to build grassroots movements that promote safe schools, racial justice, and nondiscriminatory policies. Equality Federation makes available on its website reports about its current and past projects.

Gay & Lesbian Alliance Against Defamation (GLAAD)
104 West 29th Street, 4th Floor
New York, NY 10001
(212) 629-3322
website: http://www.glaad.org

The Gay & Lesbian Alliance Against Defamation works to promote fair, accurate, and inclusive representations of LGBTQ people and events in newspapers, magazines, movies, television shows, and other media. GLAAD's website includes downloadable resources on such topics as the bisexual community, LGBTQ in film, LGBTQ issues in the American South, and guides for journalists who write about LGBTQ issues.

Gay, Lesbian and Straight Education Network (GLSEN)
110 William Street, 30th Floor
New York, NY 10038
(212) 727-0135
website: http://glsen.org

The Gay, Lesbian and Straight Education Network works to create a safe school environment for LGBTQ students and educators. It supports community action by creating local chapters throughout the US and world. The GLSEN website provides resources for students and educators such as lesson plans, professional development, and legislative proposals.

Health Professionals Advancing LGBT Equality (GLMA)
1326 18th Street NW, Suite 22
Washington, DC 20036
(202) 600-8037
email: info@glma.org
website: http://www.glma.org

GLMA is an organization that works to ensure equality in health care for lesbian, gay, bisexual, and transgender (LGBT) individuals and health care providers. The GLMA website provides resources for patients, health care providers, and students on such topics as same-sex marriage and health, treating drug addiction, and transgender health issues.

Human Rights Campaign (HRC)
1640 Rhode Island Avenue NW
Washington, DC 20036-3278
(202) 628-4160
email: feedback@hrc.org
website: http://www.hrc.org

Human Rights Campaign works to achieve LGBTQ equality and end discrimination against LGBTQ people by challenging discriminatory laws and campaigning for more inclusive legislation. HRC publishes *Equality* magazine, the nation's largest-circulation LGBTQ magazine. The website also provides a searchable database of articles and reports on topics such as marriage, dating, adoption, discrimination, and violence.

Lambda Legal
120 Wall Street, 19th Floor
New York, NY 10005-3919
(212) 809-8585
website: http://lambdalegal.org

Lambda Legal is a non-for-profit legal organization dedicated to achieving full equality for lesbian and gay people. It provides representation in court, leads public education campaigns, and advocates for public policy at all levels. Resources are available on its website on topics such as health care, employment, HIV, immigration, and police and criminal justice.

National Center for Lesbian Rights (NCLR)
870 Market Street, Suite 370
San Francisco, CA 94102
(415) 392-6257
email: Info@NCLRights.org
website: http://www.nclrights.org

The National Center for Lesbian Rights is a national legal organization committed to advancing the civil and human rights of lesbian, gay, bisexual, and transgender people and their families through litigation, legislation, policy, and public education. NCLR litigates precedent-setting cases, advocates for equitable public policies affecting the LGBT community, provides free legal assistance to LGBT people, and conducts community education on LGBT issues. Its website provides resources for LGBT youth and families.

National Center for Transgender Equality (NCTE)
1400 16th Street NW
Suite 510
Washington, DC 20036
(202) 642-4542
email: ncte@transequality.org
website: http://www.transequality.org

The National Center for Transgender Equality is a social justice advocacy organization that advocates for policy changes that improve the lives of transgender people. NCTE works to end discrimination and violence against transgender people by providing a voice in government and communities. Its website provides resources regarding identity documents and privacy, non-discrimination laws, employment, and housing and homelessness.

National LGBTQ Task Force
1325 Massachusetts Avenue NW, Suite 600
Washington, DC 20005
(202) 393-5177
website: http://www.thetaskforce.org

The National LGBTQ Task Force is a social justice not-for-profit organization that organizes the grassroots power of the lesbian, gay, bisexual, transgender, and queer community. The Task Force supports activism on behalf of LGBTQ people as well as conducting research, policy analysis, public education, and advocacy. The Task Force publishes reports and fact sheets on many current issues impacting the LGBTQ community.

PFLAG (formerly Federation of Parents and
Friends of Lesbians and Gays)
1828 L Street NW, Suite 660
Washington, DC 20036
(202) 467-8180
email: info@pflag.org
website: http://www.pflag.org

PFLAG is a not-for-profit organization that provides support for families, friends, and people who are LGBTQ. PFLAG provides educational resources and community advocacy for more than 400 chapters nationwide. Its website provides databases on hate crimes, information about transgender people, and training materials for becoming a more inclusive society.

TransLatin@ Coalition (TLC)
1730 W Olympic Boulevard, Suite 300
Los Angeles, CA 90015-1007
website: http://www.translatinacoalition.org

The mission of TransLatin@ Coalition is to advocate for the specific needs of the Trans Latin@ community that resides in the US and to plan strategies that improve their quality of life. TLC provides resources to promote the empowerment of trans leaders.

Bibliography

Books

The Associated Press — *Gay America: The Road to Gay Marriage and LGBT Rights*. New York, NY: Associated Press, 2015.

Carlos Ball — *After Marriage Equality: The Future of LGBTQ Rights*. New York, NY: New York University Press, 2016.

Ann Bausum — *Stonewall: Breaking Out in the Fight for Gay Rights*. New York, NY: Viking, 2015.

Laura A. Belmonte — *The International LGBT Rights Movement: A History*. New York, NY: Bloomsbury Academic, 2017.

Adrian Brooks — *The Right Side of History: 100 Years of LGBT Activism*. New York, NY: Cleis Press, 2015.

Kevin Cathcart and Leslie Gabel-Brett, eds. — *Love Unites Us: Winning the Freedom to Marry in America*. New York, NY: The New Press, 2016.

Debra Cenziper and James Obergefell — *Love Wins: The Lovers and Lawyers Who Fought the Landmark Case for Marriage Equality*. New York, NY: HarperCollins Publishers, 2016.

Jim Downs — *Stand by Me: The Forgotten History of Gay Liberation*. Philadelphia, PA: Basic Books, 2016.

Kerry Eleveld — *Don't Tell Me to Wait: How the Fight for Gay Rights Changed America and Transformed Obama's Presidency*. Philadelphia, PA: Basic Books, 2015.

Lillian Faderman — *The Gay Revolution: The Story of the Struggle*. New York, NY: Simon & Schuster, 2015.

Walter Frank — *Law and the Gay Rights Story: The Long Search for Equal Justice in a Divided Democracy*. New Brunswick, NJ: Rutgers Press, 2014.

Jazz Jennings	*Being Jazz: My Life as a (Transgender) Teen.* New York, NY: Crown Books for Young Readers, 2016.
Roberta Kaplan and Lisa Dickey	*Then Comes Marriage: United States v. Windsor.* New York, NY: W. W. Norton & Company, Inc., 2015.
Doug Meyer	*Violence Against Queer People: Race, Gender, and the Persistence of Anti-LGBT Discrimination.* New Brunswick, NJ: Rutgers Press, 2015.
Kevin Mumford	*Not Straight, Not White: Black Gay Men from the March on Washington to the AIDS Crisis.* Chapel Hill, NC: University of North Carolina Press, 2016.
Michelangelo Signorile	*It's Not Over: Getting Beyond Tolerance, Defeating Homophobia, and Winning True Equality.* Boston, MA: Mariner Books, 2016.
Timothy Stewart-Winter	*Queer Clout: Chicago and the Rise of Gay Politics.* Philadelphia, PA: University of Pennsylvania Press, 2016.
Cyd Zeigler	*Fair Play: How LGBT Athletes Are Claiming Their Rightful Place in Sports.* New York, NY: Akashic Books, 2015.

Periodicals and Internet Sources

Richmond Blake	"Promoting an LGBT Inclusive Human Rights Agenda," *Foreign Service Journal*, Vol. 92, Issue 5, June 2015, pp. 28–33.
Michael J. Bosia	"Strange Fruit: Homophobia, the State, and the Politics of LGBT Rights and Capabilities," *Journal of Human Rights*, Vol. 13, Issue 3, July–September 2014, pp. 256–273.
Shawn Dorman	"Human Rights for LGBT Persons: Aiming for Sustainable Progress," *Foreign Service Journal*, Vol. 92, Issue 5, June 2015, pp. 20–24.
Kerry Eleveld	"A Movement in Chaos," *Advocate*, Issue 1084, April/May 2016, pp. 34–35.

Philip Elliott	"Growing Pains for the LGBT March," *Time*, Vol. 186, Issue 27/28, December 28, 2015, pp. 60–61.
Jennifer Jigour	"LGBT Through the Ages," *USA Today Magazine*, Vol. 142, Issue 2828, May 2014, pp. 50–52.
Adele P. Kimmel	"Title IX: An Imperfect but Vital Tool to Stop Bullying of LGBT Students," *Yale Law Journal*, Vol. 125, Issue 7, May 2016, pp. 2006–2036.
Marvice D. Marcus	"The New Black: LGBT Rights and African American Communities," *Western Journal of Black Studies*, Vol. 39, Issue 1, Spring 2015, pp. 78–79.
Shane T Muñoz and David M. Kalteux	"LGBT, the EEOC, and the Meaning of 'Sex,'" *Florida Bar Journal*, Vol. 90, Issue 3, March 2016, pp. 43–48.
Kevin D. Williamson	"The Transgender Culture War," *National Review*, Vol. 68, Issue 10, June 13, 2016, pp. 30–32.

Index